Before the Scramble: A Scottish Missionary's Story
The Journal of James Sutherland, Agriculturist
Livingstonia Mission
British Central Africa, 1880–1885

By Roderick Sutherland Haynes

**HIGHLANDER PRESS
RENTON, WASHINGTON
WWW.HIGHLANDERPRESS.COM**

© 2015 by Highlander Press
ISBN 9781515380795

*This book is available for purchase from
Amazon.com, Kindle, and other retail outlets.*

The phrase "Scramble for Africa" refers to the competition (scramble) for territory between the European imperial powers in the Victorian age. The term appears in book titles—such as the one listed in the Bibliography in the back of this book—and in other professional writings about the ruthless, complex dynamics of late 19th century colonialism.

The Author

Acknowledgments

Ten years ago my mother, Helen D. Haynes of Providence, Rhode Island, gave her children faded copies of a journal written by her great uncle James Sutherland, who was a Scottish missionary in British Central Africa in the 1880s. While researching Sutherland's personal history and the Victorian period in general over the past two years, I read several books written by individuals Sutherland met and interacted with on the 'dark continent.' Some of these books were helpful to me in my efforts to know the man and his time and situation, others not so much.

Transcribing Sutherland's journal was not easy, but it was great fun and often fascinating. There were situations where two or more witnesses attending the same event (example: the baptism of Albert at the Livingstonia mission at Bandawe in the spring of 1881 — the first baptism held there) capture their impressions in writing. Reading multiple accounts of a specific situation gave me a balanced perspective on what actually went on.

My research led me to a number of interesting people, including Professor Joanna Lewis of the London School of Economics, Professor John McCracken of the University of Stirling in Scotland, and Professor Adrian

Wisnicki of the University of Nebraska at Lincoln. Each one of them graciously lent me their advice and encouragement.

Mr. Harry Gray, Chairperson of the Wick Society of Wick, Scotland recommended several useful resources and points of contact. Mark Totten of Seattle WA provided excellent copy-editing service and writing advice (contact: mark@commadash.com). Two dear friends, John Andrew of Renton, WA and Dr. Alvah Bittner of Kent, WA offered their thoughts and encouragement. Mas Yamamoto of Renton, WA contributed the author's photograph gracing the back cover of this book, for which I am truly grateful.

Work colleague Dr. Nancy Fisher graciously offered me her insight about tropical diseases specific to the African continent. Another colleague, Dr. Holly Robinson, generously edited a near-final edition of this project, offering valuable pointers. I thank them both.

Pride in Sutherland clan history clearly runs deep on both sides of the Atlantic Ocean. Relatives Roger and Helen Craik of Edinburgh, Scotland offered extremely valuable photographs and background information. My love and thankfulness, as always, goes out to Mom, my son Ben Haynes of NY City, and to my siblings Libby, Seth, and Holly. I am very grateful to artist (and new stepdaughter) Katie Kurkjy of Seattle, WA for her artistic rendering (a hand-drawn map) of "James Sutherland's World" on page xvii. Terrific stuff, really.

We are separated from James Sutherland and his world by more than 130 years. I often found myself wishing I could talk to him, as there are many questions that remain unanswered. I feel privileged even to have *attempted* to bring this slice of history alive, for the sake of family members who may have interest in Sutherland's story, as well as for professional historians seeking new primary sources related to the early colonial period in Africa. I documented as many sources as I possibly could in putting this project together. These sources are listed in the bibliography.

Finally, to my best friend, confidante, and new wife, Daria, you will always have my deepest love and gratitude for your editing advice, graphic design expertise, and emotional support over the past two years. It's time to grab a beer and celebrate. I'm done.

Rod Haynes

"History is always written by the winners. When two cultures clash, the loser is obliterated, and the winner writes the history books-books which glorify their own cause and disparage the conquered foe. As Napoleon once said, 'What is history, but a fable agreed upon?'"

—Dan Brown, *The Da Vinci Code*

James Sutherland of Wick, Scotland

"The normative early nineteenth century missionary was a working man. To describe him as a member of the lower class would be to mislead. He was an artisan, a worker with a skill, and even such clergy as went were seldom of a different background . . . He had been well educated, no doubt, but he had been to no university and had acquired his honorary doctorate by kind arrangement of Princeton . . . . As missionaries, many had little, if any, training, education and theology were rather pointless. What was needed was a good knowledge of the Bible, a great deal of faith, and a strong voice."

—Adrian Hastings, *The Church In Africa: 1450–1950,* © 1996, p.10

Table of Contents

Prologue

In the spring of 1966 my sixth-grade classmates and I stood inside a brightly colored, stained glass globe towering over our heads. The *Mapparium* in downtown Boston was built in 1935 with 600 individually shaped pieces of rippled glass joined together, forming an expansive walk-in sphere. We were encased in the most amazing object I'd ever seen—a snapshot of the world as it existed between World War I and World War II. The walkway's height was level with the globe's equator. We stood looking at its curved glass imperfectly speckled by thousands of tiny air bubbles, I pointed out several multicolored continents and deep blue oceans to my friend, Brad. "Holy Cow," I murmured, "this thing's a thousand times bigger than Mr. Smith's globe back at school." Brad responded, "Yeah, but look, this one's not tilting over like his does. It's standin' straight up and down." Our attention fell on Africa's BELGIAN CONGO, FRENCH WEST AFRICA, and NYASALAND, those former colonies' dark black lettering highlighted by brilliantly hued backgrounds of green, blue, orange, yellow, and red glass.

I lingered inside the *Mapparium* for a long time that afternoon, oblivious to the injuries inflicted on Africa and her peoples by their European conquerors in the name of God, King, and Country. Years later I discovered a direct ancestral connection to the "Scramble for Africa" through a personal journal which taught me that the story of colonialism is far more complicated than how standard history texts tell it.

By the end of the 19th century, the imperialists controlled more than 10 million of the 11.5 million total square miles of Africa.[1] And while debates continue about when the Victorian period's Scramble for Africa began and ended, it is generally

---

[1]   *Dawn in the Dark Continent*, Dr. James Stewart, p. 17.

acknowledged colonialism helped ignite two cataclysmic world wars—and countless smaller subsequent conflicts. Parts of Africa are still plagued by violence from seeds planted more than a century ago. The imperialists neither invented war nor did they import war into what was otherwise a peaceful land. Violence in many cruel forms was ingrained in African tribal cultures long before the "white man" appeared there to make the killing of humans and wildlife more lethally efficient than ever before imagined. And not all European conquerors wore military uniforms. Missionaries and commercial traders played unique roles in the long, bloody drama in late 19th century Africa.

The hero of our story was a devout servant of God—a brave young Scotsman-turned-African-missionary. Sent by his church in 1880, he served in a distant land where rival tribes inflicted brutal atrocities on each other, wild animals prowled local villages devouring the unwary, and virulent tropical diseases wiped away the lives of victims. Like today, some missionaries back then agreed to serve without fully grasping the risks involved, no doubt seeking adventure or, perhaps, escape from their mundane lives at home. Others were willing to lay down their lives in the name of Jesus Christ, as Scotland's greatest 19th century medical missionary-explorer hero, Dr. David Livingstone, had done before them. The missionaries were part of multiple diasporas happening at once, a massive population movement out of Britain, Ireland, Scotland, and other parts of Western Europe in the middle of the 19th century, bound for different corners of the globe, including America.

"Between the Battle of Waterloo and the end of the American Civil War in 1865 the British empire grew by an average of

100,000 miles per year. . . part of their success was due to the fact that most immigrants, even the poorest, had more skills and education than their European counterparts. This broad-based 'brain drain' was bad news for Scotland over the long haul, but good news for the rest of the world."[2]

James Sutherland found his courage through faith, trusting that, "God would provide," wherever his new life would take him. Though his faith and courage would be sorely tested in a number of ways, Sutherland would not be deterred from performing his duties, leaving his own unique imprint on the world before his brief time on earth ended.

---

[2] *How the Scots Invented the Modern World*, Arthur Herman, Three Rivers Press NY, NY, 2001, pp. 346-347.

James Sutherland, Missionary

James Sutherland, my maternal great-grandfather's brother, was the second oldest of four sons. He was born in 1857 in the midst of a powerful religious revival sweeping Europe. Scotland was, "going through an unabashed phase of 'being born again.' Protestant sects such as Congregationalists, Baptists, and Methodists found eager converts among Scotland's rural and urban workers. Shops, taverns, even most city services, strictly observed the Sabbath—a custom that persisted until very recently."[3]

Sutherland was a classic product of this post-Scottish Enlightenment environment, the son of an ordinary shoemaker from Wick, a tiny seaside village in Scotland's Upper Highlands. Dr. Walter Angus Elmslie, an early family friend and later a mission colleague, wrote in his book that Sutherland accepted Christ around the age of 17. Elmslie further reported in *Among the Wild Ngoni* that Sutherland's conversion took place at a Free Church of Scotland revival headlined by Henry Drummond, one of the "Scottish lieutenants" working for American evangelist Dwight L. Moody.[4] Moody may have been present to hear Sutherland's profession of faith, though it cannot be confirmed he was actually there.

---

[3] *How the Scots Invented the Modern World*, Arthur Herman, Three Rivers Press NY, NY, 2001, pp. 377-378.

[4] Dwight L. Moody may be considered late-19th century America's equivalent to today's Billy Graham.

Success with his early schooling brought the studious Sutherland a bursary (scholarship) award from the University of Edinburgh. An active church member involved in evangelical outreach, Sutherland considered becoming a missionary after completing his studies. At the end of his second university session, a missionary's sudden death in southeastern Africa presented the young man with an unexpected missionary opportunity. Sutherland interviewed for the vacancy and, after being offered the job by the Free Church of Scotland's Foreign Missions Committee, left England in November 1880 to bring the Word of God to Africa.[5] A strong sense of nationalistic pride, mixed with an evangelical commitment to service, gripped the British Empire after the death of Scottish medical missionary-explorer hero David Livingstone in the spring of 1873 and his subsequent internment at Westminster Abbey. (Livingstone's heart had been buried in Africa, the rest of his remains were then shipped back to England.) Scores of young Scots like Sutherland dreamed of emulating Livingstone's achievements in Africa, or, perhaps, pursuing work in India or China.

The Disruption of 1843 saw the Free Church of Scotland split from the Church of Scotland, "during a period of rapid transformation when a predominantly rural community of landed proprietors and peasantry was giving way to an industrial society with wide divisions between classes and as Scotland became absorbed into an imperial society with less national identity."[6]

---

[5] A full chapter on Sutherland's life is found in *Among the Wild Ngoni*, Walter A. Elmslie, Fleming H. Revell Co. publisher, 1899, pp. 209–252.

[6] *The Letters of Jane Elizabeth Waterson, 1866–1905*, Jane E. Waterson, The Van Riebeeck Society, 1983, p. 5.

As the Industrial Revolution gained momentum, millions of western Europeans immigrated to North America or Australia.

The lack of social mobility, the advent of new technologies supplanting manual labor in the heavy industries resulting in harsher economic times, explosive population growth, and cruel environmental conditions such as the potato famine in Ireland and elsewhere in the 1840s all prompted millions of Europeans to search for better lives abroad.

For many adventurers, the end came quickly. Between 1861 and 1865 thousands of male immigrants in the United States—a good many Irish and German—died in the holocaust of the American Civil War. More than a few first-generation Scottish immigrants were also ensnared in that hellish conflict. Other Scotsmen helped expand the British Empire's global influence as members of the Royal Navy and British expeditionary land forces. A far smaller number of young men (and very few females) left home to spread the Word of God in distant places like India, China, and Africa.

Sutherland was not ordained and would never become a high-ranking official in the church hierarchy. He understood his role to be a solitary servant for Christ working alongside his peers. On the cover of his journal, Sutherland refers to himself as an "agriculturist," one artisan among teams of artisans serving at their respective missions, far from home. These artisans were engineers (shipboard and civil engineers), seamen, agriculturists (gardeners), blacksmiths, carpenters, and the like who were typically led by ordained ministers assigned to missions by individual church Foreign Missions Committees.

James Sutherland walked into an extremely unstable situation at the dawn of the African colonial period. Early on there were relatively few other Europeans to keep him company, but he did not complain, determined as he was to serve God even in the most difficult circumstances. Though he agreed to serve as an agriculturist, Sutherland quickly wound up working a variety of daily tasks at Livingstonia at Bandawe. The artisans were specialists, but they performed many different tasks to keep their missions functioning.

Three letters Sutherland sent home to Scotland survived. He described close calls with wild beasts, as well as the tedium of mission life.[7] He spent his days overseeing the building of roads, learning languages, planting gardens, and supervising native work teams of gardeners, carpenters, and joiners (wood workers). Each Sabbath he attended church services offered in native languages before attending English services. Well into his third year in Africa Sutherland wrote to his father:

> "I am only a teacher in name. In reality I am a bricklayer & house builder for that is the kind of work at which I am engaged, and have been working at since I came into the country."[8]

All sorts of questions cropped up as my research moved forward. How did Sutherland cope with the many native languages—at least 15 different dialects were spoken in the vicinity of Livingstonia—while mediating tribal conflicts against

---

[7] See Appendix II.

[8] Appendix II, Sutherland's first letter home dated August 15, 1882.

explicit instructions of the church mission's sponsors back home, fending off threats of violence by Arab slave traders, and competing with the other missions to save the souls of indifferent 'heathens'? How were tribal disputes—the potential for violence a constant concern—mediated by the missionaries? How much overlap was there between the goals of the missions (church) and those of the various Foreign Service Offices (international politics)? What were the differences? Where did attempts at converting the tribal members and engaging in politics with them begin and end? Organizers of the Berlin Conference of 1884 did not invite any African leaders, making it clear the Africans were not considered worthy of inclusion. Did the missionaries treat tribal members as human beings or savages?

Sutherland's original journal is now the property of the National Library of Scotland. His role was not pivotal in the drama of Victorian colonialism. However, he crossed paths with people who *were* crucial players in feeding the British Empire's appetite for new territory and raw materials. In this respect, Sutherland's journal presents an abbreviated yet still detailed picture of the everyday lives of the early Christian missionaries. Not many journals of his time and place are known to exist today.

Historians point to the Berlin Conference of 1884 as the start of the Scramble for Africa. Did this watershed Conference impact Sutherland? Missionaries, explorers, commercial traders and Foreign Office officials from one country operated in close proximity to one other. What framed the relationships between these competing entities? One example of cooperation was the Livingstonia missionaries giving their steamship *Ilala* to the African Lakes Company, permitting the Company to build their local commercial ties while shuttling the missionaries around Lake Nyasa and nearby waterways. Over time there was growing cooperation between the missions of different faiths, between the missions and commercial interests, and between the missions and the Foreign Service Offices of their respective countries back home. At the same time, numerous unforeseen complications emerged in the early scramble years. The tribal members tried building bi-lateral alliances with a number of these entities, hoping to exclude their enemies in the process. And like the Native Americans in the western U.S. at that time, African tribal chiefs did not fully grasp the ramifications of signing pieces of papers (treaties) their European partners considered legally binding.

Sutherland undoubtedly understood hardships awaited him in Africa when he set sail—he was replacing a young man who had died in country from an unidentified sickness that claimed many fellow Europeans. Like many missionaries, Sutherland kept a personal journal, but it is unlikely he intended to publish it in the future. As he made his way north on the Zambesi and Shire Rivers towards his destination at Livingstonia, Sutherland wrote entries in his journal and read Livingstone's accounts of Africa while passing by landmarks— including the grave site of Mrs. Livingstone. Sutherland's duties and never-ending struggles with poor health probably explain why he did not keep his journal current. It is genuine and, for the most part, lacking the self-flattery and haughtiness typical of Victorian literature. Inescapably a product of his time, Sutherland's views may appear to be condescending in certain entries, to modern eyes. But his kind, gentle soul permeates the journal, accompanied by a self-deprecating sense of humor. He clearly knew and liked himself. Sutherland's cheerful disposition, calm courage, and unshakeable faith carried him through more than a few hair-raising situations, including a terrible ritual ordered by a native chief that came close to ending his life.[9] Sutherland faced danger everywhere—mysteriously chronic jungle diseases, hostile tribal members, constant weather extremes, lack of food and poor sanitation, relentless attacks by mosquitoes and fire ants and deadly tsetse flies, groups of lions and packs of hyenas and rampaging elephants, swarms of crocodiles and threatening hippopotamus'—all part of daily life in Africa.

If Sutherland could have foreseen the results of the Berlin Conference of 1884, would he have gone to Africa in the first place? There is no way of knowing the answer. Returning home was not an attractive option for Sutherland; times continued to be hard there. In his September 20, 1883 letter to his brother John— he was two years younger—James wrote:

> "I heard last mail that you were thinking of going to Australia. I can by no means find fault with you though father says that you can rise in Glasgow as well as in a foreign land. . . Your case [i.e., whether or not to leave Scotland] is different from mine. I set out to a place cut and ready for me so that I had no dark thoughts of what I was to do. But on the other hand you are going out in a sense not knowing where are going or what you are to do, so therefore you will leave home with very different feelings from me. I was never happier in all my life than

---

9   Appendix II, Sutherland's first letter home dated August 15, 1882.

when I launched forth on the broad ocean and the same happiness continues to this very day unbroken and undisturbed."[10]

A year later, in his September 1884 letter to John, (who had, during that year, emigrated to America, not Australia) James briefly mentions their youngest brother Dugald:

"I wonder what he is like now. Has he grown much? I fear he will be but dwarfish at best. You see what his poor upbringing on tea has done for him. I am glad I got a start in growth before the hard pinching days came, and they were really hard. I can afford to cry out against them now but not then. 'Hard times come again no more.'"[11]

Sadly, Dugald died within the next year. The Sutherland family had experienced losses prior to Dugald: apparently both James Sutherland's mother and her newborn baby died in childbirth in 1865.[12] John Sutherland, who listed himself as a dry goods clerk on his citizenship naturalization papers issued in Providence, Rhode Island in 1896, became my mother's grandfather.

In the end, James Sutherland's journal successfully reaches across time. It is a source of pride for his descendants. Though few individuals beyond members of my family know of its existence, the journal could be one useful resource to historians focusing on the early colonial period in British Central Africa. This is an intriguing tale told by an ordinary gardener

---

[10] Appendix II, Sutherland's second letter dated September 20, 1883.
[11] Appendix II, Sutherland's third letter, dated September, 1882.
[12] Details about the death of James' mother and brother are unclear.

under extraordinary circumstances. Historically significant or not, the journal's authenticity resonates with us. It teaches us. We are drawn to James Sutherland—a dedicated servant of God in Africa—before imperialism made its own imprint there. At the same time we should bear in mind the tragic drama in Africa today owes its problems, at least partially, to events James Sutherland unwittingly helped shape as an artisan at the first and second Livingstonia missions on Lake Nyasa in the mid 1880s.

The Pre-Scramble: Maps and Missionaries

Since Scottish missionary-explorer David Livingstone arrived in southeastern Africa in the 1840s, the borders of modern day Malawi have been drawn and redrawn countless times. Parts of this region have been labeled (to name but a few), "Portuguese Territory," "Upper Shire," "Lake Nyasa Region," "protectorate of British Central Africa," "British Central Africa," and "Nyasa-land." Even the spelling of geographic landmarks and villages on charts, maps, and period books is markedly inconsistent over time: "Nyassa" verses "Nyasa," "Quellimane" verses "Quilimane," and so forth. The Victorian era's mapping of the African continent has been described this way:

> ". . .the arbitrary nature of much colonial map-making . . . conferences and diplomatic maneuverings [that] in European capitals often drew lines to deal with the tensions among the colonizing powers rather than addressing internal African issues . . . they imposed outwardly oriented development patterns upon the continent. [Resulting in the] ' Balkinization' into numerous territories of varying sizes rather than a few big units . . ."[13]

For consistency, I will be referring to the area west and south of Lake Nyasa—now called Lake Malawi—as British Central Africa in the knowledge that the territorial labels on

---

[13] *Mapping Africa: Problems of Regional Definition and Colonial/National Boundaries.* See http://fathom.lib.uchicago.edu, p.3.

contemporary charts during colonialism and afterwards, were always in flux. Most of this area was proclaimed a British protectorate in 1889, before formal ratification came in 1891.

Regarding the presence of local missions, the situation in British Central Africa by 1880 has been described as, "an unplanned multiplicity of organizations often overlapping on the ground, co-operative in part but also jealous of one another's influence, anxious that their own church rather than another should prevail . . . [missions included] British Methodists and Anglicans, Scottish Presbyterians, American Congregationalists, French Calvinists, and Norwegian Lutherans . . ."[14] The mission labels, "Livingstonia I, II, and III" on the map on page xvii are my creation. They show the progression of the three separate Free Church of Scotland missions on Lake Nyasa (it is 300 miles long): the first one at the far southern end at Cape Maclear in 1875 (Livingstonia I), then at Bandawe on the lakes' mid-western shoreline in 1881 (Livingstonia II) and, finally, at a settlement north of Florence Bay on a high plateau set back from the northwest coastline of Lake Nyasa in the mid 1890s (Livingstonia III). When the missionaries departed a mission, trusted tribal members were left in charge of what we would call a 'satellite site.' How and why these site changes took place is an important sub-plot in our story. A founder of Livingstonia I at Cape Maclear, recalled his first impression of the proposed site:

---

[14] *The Church in Africa, 1450 – 1950*, Adrian Hastings, Oxford Scholarship online, 2003, p. 37.

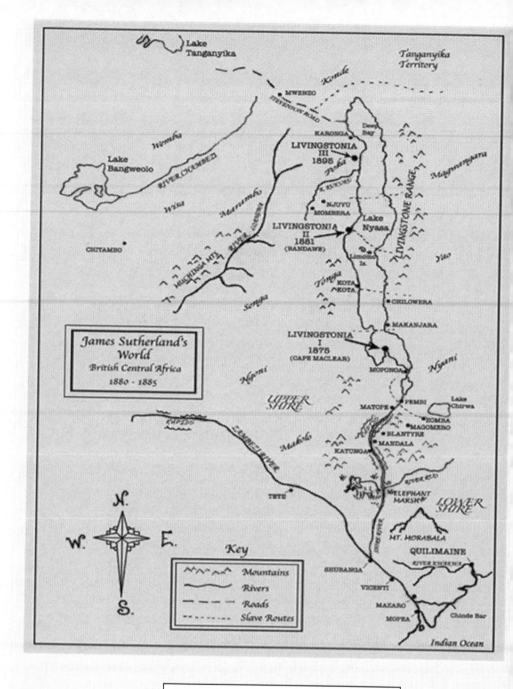

Lake Tanganyika

Tanganyika Territory

Komle

MWENZO

STEVENSON ROAD

KARONGA

Deep Bay

Wemba

RIVER COLUMBEI

Lake Bangweolo

LIVINGSTONIA III 1895

Peruku

Marumbo

N. KUKUKU

NJUYU

MOMBERA

LIVINGSTONIA II 1881 (BANDAWE)

Lake Nyasa

LIVINGSTONE RANGE

Mbyamapara

Yao

CHITAMBO

RIVER COMBEI

HUCHINGA MTS

LIKOMA Is.

Tonga

KOTA KOTA

CHILOWERA

MAKANJARA

Senga

LIVINGSTONIA I 1875 (CAPE MACLEAR)

MPONGA

Nyani

James Sutherland's World
British Central Africa
1880 - 1885

Nyani

UPPER SHIRE

MATOPE

PEMBI

Lake Chirwa

SOMBA

MAGOMERO

BLANTYRE

MANDALA

Makolo

KAPENA

ZAMBEZI RIVER

KATUNGA

TETE

ELEPHANT MARSH

SHIRE RIVER

LOWER SHIRE

N.

W. E.

S.

MT. MORABALA

QUILIMAINE

RIVER KWAKWA

SHUBANGA

VICENTI

MAZARO

MOPEA

Chinde Bar

Key

~~~~~ Mountains
⌇⌇⌇⌇ Rivers
— — — Roads
· — · — Slave Routes

Indian Ocean

SCALE: LAKE NYASA IS
APPROX. 300 MILES LONG

xvii

"It was a lonely land of barbarism, of game, and wild beasts, of not unkindly men, harassed by never-ending slave raids and inter-tribal wars."[15]

The roster of the 38 mission personnel assigned to the Livingstonia missions and their satellites between 1875 and 1890 tells a grim story: roughly 40 percent of the staff died or incurred serious health problems before their time in Africa ended.[16] The criteria for selecting a mission site included: (1) a suitable harbor for a steamship landing, delivery, and transport; (2) good soil to grow crops; (3) abundant timber in the immediate vicinity for construction projects; and (4) plenty of fresh water had to be readily available.[17] The importance for a proposed mission site to be a low-threat disease spot arose only after harsh lessons had been learned at Livingstonia I. Cape Maclear topography mostly consisted of low-level swamp land surrounded on three sides by steep mountain slopes, draining water into the flat land below. In summary, the first Livingstonia mission proved to be a perfect breeding ground for malaria and other deadly sicknesses.

Though missionary life was hard for young Europeans like Sutherland, serving God overseas remained an attractive alternative to their bleak prospects at home. Not all volunteers for Victorian era missionary work in Africa, India, and China loved God in their hearts. In James Sutherland's case, however, the evidence confirms his commitment to God was genuine. As for Sutherland's peers, some turned to commercial pursuits once

---

15 *Dawn in the Dark Continent*, Dr. James Stewart, p. 209.

16 Appendix III

17 *Daybreak In Livingstonia*, J.W. Jack, p.140.

they landed overseas, a small number became criminals (the tribal members tended to quickly dispatch those committing particularly egregious offenses), and others, if not succumbing to disease, gave up and left. There were missionaries who fulfilled their obligations and returned home to write books about their adventures hoping to strike it rich. A few brave souls dutifully remained at their posts far beyond what they had agreed to in the beginning.[18]

A modern historian writes: "a frequently recurring problem was the interrelationships of missionaries among themselves. They had not been trained for community, or to share a common work; they tended to be individualistic and obstinate by temperament; they often quarreled fearfully."[19] Sutherland's journal confirms he encountered problems of this sort at the missions where he lived. That aside, in the years leading to the scramble, the Scottish missionaries focused on "developing the potential of human nature through education and evangelism."[20] They insisted tribal members conform to worshiping God the European way, become civilized as Europeans defined civilization, and conduct commerce in

---

[18] Dr. Robert Laws, the sole ordained minister assigned to Livingstonia I at the outset, was a United Presbyterian not religiously affiliated with the Free Church of Scotland, sponsor of Livingstonia. Laws served in the Lake Nyasa area for 52 years. By the time his service ended Laws was highly regarded by area tribal leaders and many of his European peers.

[19] *The Church in Africa 1450–1950*, Adrian Hastings, 1996, p. 253.

[20] *The Origins and Early Development of Scottish Presbyterianism in South Africa (1824–1865)*, Graham A. Duncan, Department of Church History and Polity, University of Pretoria, Pretoria, South Africa. See last paragraph on page 2 of the abstract.

accordance with European practices. Livingstonia I mission founder and leader Robert Laws recognized that Christian leaders should be cultivated from within the ranks of the tribes, a progressive attitude at the time, but conformity to Victorian mores was still at the core of the missionary movement. Laws conducted vocational training, simultaneously evangelizing to skeptical tribal members. Language barriers remained a big problem for a long time, but Laws taught himself several dialects enabling him to better reach his 'flock.' Laws developed native church leaders because there were few European ministers and volunteers to expand outreach missions. Other missions did the same thing, but somehow Laws' efforts attracted more attention from politicians back home and from his peers, probably because he was one of the first to experiment in this manner. The competition between the Free Church of Scotland and other denominations (most notably the Roman Catholic missions) intensified as the scramble gained momentum in the mid 1880s.

The imperialist powers carefully maintained the facade that their reason for coming to Africa was to crush the slave trade and establish new commercial opportunities in its place but the force of international politics quickly established itself in many parts of Africa. Though missionaries like Robert Laws and James Sutherland were sincere in their attempts to convert 'heathens,' the tribal members increasingly felt the cruel military heels of their new masters as the international competition for land and influence became the top priority. It is no small irony that the missionaries made greater progress converting the tribal members after the scramble brought the locals in line through more persuasive means than prayer and good will alone. But the constant presence and persistence of the missionaries also improved conversion rates as the 20th century drew closer.

The area south and east of British Central Africa was labeled 'Portuguese Territory' on most European charts. Much of this area later became Mozambique. At one time it served as a penal colony for Portugal's hardened criminals, similar to Britain's exporting a large percentage of their criminal population to Australia. Arab slave traders working in close proximity to the missions in British Central Africa hired Portuguese convicts and their descendants, causing recurring headaches for the evangelicals who were prohibited by their churches from taking sides in what often became volatile disputes. The map on page xvii reflects approximate tribal locations and slave routes on Lake Nyasa in Sutherland's time.

Conflict between the slave traders and fledgling European commercial interests escalated in the late 1880s. The slave traders saw the missions and European traders for what they were: direct threats to their enterprises. The imperialists' respective Foreign Service Offices (FSOs) eventually hired local militia to solidify their respective country's sovereignty in their areas of interest. These actions sent a clear message to the competing powers intent on staking out their own claims. In the Lake Nyasa region protracted competition between Britain and Portugal over boundary / sovereignty issues almost led to open conflict before the matter was settled by negotiation at the Berlin Conference of 1884.

Native resistance to their new colonial masters intensified as political, economic, and religious upheaval in British Central Africa (and in many other parts of Africa) became the new norm.[21] By the time the scramble was over, the winners (the imperialists) could thank emerging technologies, new medicinal discoveries, and employment of modern weaponry for subduing the losers (the Africans). Steam ships (civilian transport and military gunships) and telegraphs, reliance on quinine to treat symptoms of malaria, and the presence of new mechanized weaponry—oddly sometimes given as gifts to tribal chiefs—were mentioned in Sutherland's journal. Progress in connecting strategic and commercial centers through new railroad lines, and more broadly, in connecting the west and east coasts of Africa, came more quickly in the 1890s when rapid movement of troops and cargo became essential to the imperial powers' plans.

In spite of missionaries, explorers, and entrepreneurs operating close to their villages, the tribal members refused to set aside inter-tribal rivalries, attempting to forge alliances against their enemies and demonstrating jealousy when the missionaries continued to welcome all visitors to their compounds regardless of tribal affiliation. The missionaries did this to emphasize God's love of all people.

---

[21] Machemba, king of the local Yao tribe, told German commander, Hermann von Wissman, in 1890: "I have listened to your words but can find no reason why I should obey you—I would rather die first . . .If it should be friendship that you desire, then I am ready for it, today and always, but to be your subject, that I cannot be . . .If it should be war you desire, then I am ready, but never to be your subject . . .I do not fall at your feet, for you are God's creature just as I am . . .I am Sultan here in my land. You are Sultan there in yours. Yet Listen, I do not say to you that you should obey me; for I know that you are free man . . .As for me, I will not come to you, and if you are not strong enough, then come and fetch me." *African Perspectives on Colonialism*, A. Adu Boahen, 1987, pp.23-24.

The demographics of the tribes living near Lake Nyasa in Sutherland's time were extremely complex and fluid. The Makolo tribe lived in the Upper Shire region near the Blantyre Mission. Their connection to Blantyre and Livingstonia went back to Livingstone, whom the Makolo's highly regarded, having received gifts (including guns) from Livingstone to help cement their support of his work. Sutherland's group employed Makolos as porters on the River Shire before they turned against the missionaries as the older generation died off.[22]

The Ngonis, direct descendants of the Zulus, were considered by the missionaries to be the most war-like tribe around Lake Nyasa, having migrated to the northern region of the lake from South Africa in the early 1800s. The Ngonis targeted the Tongas and the Yaos. The Yaos, in turn, allied with local Arab slave raiders to wreak havoc on weaker tribes like the Manganjas and Wakonde.[23]

The Tongas, bitter rivals of the Ngoni Zulu, resided on the western shoreline of Lake Nyasa in cliff areas difficult to access by local raiding tribes (see map on page xvii). The European public was not aware that the slave trade continued in parts of Africa until the end of the 19th century (and beyond, in places like the Belgium Congo). The political double-speak of

---

[22] A detailed review of inter-tribal conflicts and various alliances with the missionaries and Arab slave traders is found in *British Central Africa: The Territories Under British Influence North of the Zambesi*, Sir Harry H. Johnston, Methuen & Co., London, 1903. pp. 66-79.

[23] Appendix I is a brief overview of the major tribes living around Lake Nyasa in Sutherland's time. The locations of tribes showing on the map on page xvii are a composite, taken from a variety of contemporary charts and descriptions in reference documents included in the Bibliography.

the colonial powers—part of everyday business in international politics—was predictably blatant, given the paternalistic attitudes Victorians held toward native Africans and other Third World peoples throughout that period. There were certain exceptions, such as Dr. Laws, but most primary source material clearly reflects the condescending attitudes the vast majority of Victorians held towards African tribal peoples.

David Livingstone

> "It was not the desire for empire or profits that finally
> opened up Africa, but another powerful force in the
> Scottish cultural repertoire: religion. A single man did it,
> not to enrich himself or to plant the Union Jack on
> another distant shore, but for the Africans themselves, to
> bring them education, medicine, freedom from the threat
> of slavery—in other words 'civilization' in enlightened
> Scottish terms—as well as Christianity. His name was
> David Livingstone . . ."[24]

During his first visit to Africa in October 1841, David
Livingstone saw the slave trade and its horrors up close,
convincing him that human trafficking, an integral part of the
local economy in and around Lake Nyasa, must be eradicated.
Livingstone wrote graphically about mutilated bodies (the
victims of slave raids) clogging the Zambesi and Shire Rivers,
villages burned to the ground with human bones scattered
around, and the unspeakably cruel treatment of slaves by their
Arab and Portuguese captors. These raiders wiped out entire
villages to maintain the flow of slaves to the east coast for further
transport to regions north and east of Africa. Slaves owned by
children could be killed on a whim by their young owners. Those
who became old and burdensome were left as food for the lions

---

[24] A modern historian echoes the sentiments of David Livingstone's 19th
century admirers: *How the Scots Invented the Modern World*, Arthur
Herman, Three Rivers Press NY, NY, 2001, pp. 376.

and hyenas lurking around the villages at night. When tribal chieftains died hundreds of slaves could be slaughtered to accompany their masters into the next world.[25] Slaves in transit deemed too young or infirm to work were simply tossed into the brush or tied to trees by the slave traders, again left as food for the wildlife who trailed slave caravans, waiting for such opportunities. In short, slaves, while considered valuable property, lived extremely perilous lives. First-hand accounts of slave raids and their impacts on the victims are extremely graphic, leaving little to the imagination.[26]

Back in England, Livingstone's public speeches stressed replacing the African slave trade with the "3-Cs": Christianity, Commerce, and Culture. As a natural complement to the growing abolitionist movement in mid century Europe, his efforts gained traction. Livingstone envisioned local missions establishing attractive, workable, and permanent alternatives to slave trading. The missions would offer viable trade and individual skill opportunities by fusing western European culture, technology, and religion with local African labor, while taking advantage of the continent's vast untapped natural resources. Africa could also provide abundant quantities of agricultural products for the hungry masses in Europe's burgeoning urban centers. Later, in the 1870s and 1880s, the Christian missions tried implementing variations of the 3-Cs, with moderate success.[27]

---

[25] *Daybreak in Livingstonia*, Dr. James W. Jack, pp. 78-79.

[26] Ibid, pp. 17-18.

[27] A modern historian writes: "In the middle decades of the 19th century almost everyone linked together Christianity and Civilisation [sic], adding—when occasion served—Commerce or Cultivation. These Cs

A contemporary medical missionary wrote admiringly of Livingstone: "It was David Livingstone, a self-educated Scottish weaver, who, inspired with passion to discover the secret sources of the Nile, and the mysteries of Central Africa, was raised up by God to carry the Gospel message to those who, for centuries, had sat in darkness and in the shadow of death."[28] Raising Livingstone to sainthood status similar to how the vanquished Confederacy in the United States elevated General Robert E. Lee in the same historical period, English newspapers told of Livingstone being discovered dead inside his tent on his knees in a position of prayer. Accurate or not, reports of this kind resonated with British Victorians who, in spite of sharp theological differences that accompany heightened revivalism, considered their relationship to God and Jesus Christ paramount. A central theme of the fundamentalist revivals in mid 19th century Europe was an enhanced focus on converting non-believers locally (in rural and urban areas), while supporting overseas Christian missions. Protestant denominations around Western Europe thought and acted the same way.

It is important to reiterate that James Sutherland saw himself as an ambassador for Christ, modeling himself after David Livingstone. But Livingstone's role seems more complex, at least during his final years in Africa. As a young man

---

need some sorting out, if they are not to mislead. They represented the public values of the Victorian age together with Science, for 'Civilisation and Science' could as easily be linked as 'Civilisation and Commerce.' In fact, in these four terms Christianity was really the odd man out."
Victorian Scholarship On-Line, p. 23.

[28] *Among the Wild Ngoni*, Walter A. Elmslie, 1900, Introduction.

Livingstone aspired to be a medical missionary in China, but with the opium wars raging there he instead went on to win lasting fame exploring the interior of Africa. Late in life, although he continued proselytizing to tribal members, Livingstone dedicated much of his time looking for the source of the Nile River. At one point he disappeared for two years, resulting in the infamous quote ascribed to Henry Stanley, an American glory hound sent to Africa by a New York newspaper to track Livingstone down.

Livingstone's search for the Nile's is a good example of the British Empire's attempts at building an inland waterway connecting southern Africa to the newly completed Suez Canal. This grand vision likely went unrealized for two major reasons: (1) the progress in building railroad lines as the 19th century ended lessened the need for an inland waterway; and (2) the geopolitical jostling between Britain, Germany, Belgium, and the other powers in Africa left key areas needed to complete this ambitious project permanently in the hands of rivals. Acquiring new territory naturally became more difficult as the competition between the European powers heated up.

Accounts of British and Scottish explorers in Africa before the scramble, "exerted an incalculable influence on British culture and the course of modern history."[29] A famous legend told about a large lion attacking and nearly killing Livingstone. His arm was badly mangled—it was crippled for life—before the

---

29 *Victorians and Africans: The Genealogy of the Myth of the Dark Continent*, Critical Inquiry 12, Autumn 1985, Patrick Brantlinger, The University of Chicago Press, p. 176.

animal was finally brought down. The incident made Livingstone an instant hero among tribal members witnessing the attack, while galvanizing legions of Livingstone followers at home.

Two final points about Livingstone's legacy in Africa in the mid 19th century—bias as they may be—follow:

> "The one service Livingstone could bring to Africa's heartland himself was his medical practice. Livingstone became truly the first 'doctor without borders,' traveling thirty or forty miles out of his way to visit whatever village or people needed his assistance. Livingstone brought the sharp analysis and technical knowledge of Scottish medicine to some of the remotest places in the world. . . Like most Scots Livingstone was largely immune to racial theories of white supremacy (belief in white cultural supremacy was another matter). In one colonial setting after another, Scots proved themselves far better able to get along with people of another culture and color than their English counterparts. In addition, the whole weight of the Scottish Enlightenment tradition was on the side of the belief in a universal human nature, which all human beings shared. . ."[30]

An objective interpretation of missionary journals and other 19th century writings about African cultures does not fully support the suggestion that Scottish missionaries in general were less prone to prejudice. Again, the most pervasive tone in the contemporary

---

[30] *How the Scots Invented the Modern World*, Arthur Herman, Three Rivers Press NY, NY, 2001, p. 381.

literature researched for this project is paternalistic, with the missionaries (and other Europeans) acting as benevolent supervisors of "ignorant, unchurched" tribal members. In fairness some primary source material (including sources in this book's Bibliography) contains surprisingly progressive attitudes. Sutherland confirmed Dr. Robert Laws stressed teaching, while encouraging tribal members to help other natives in spiritual, educational, and practical living and working matters in and around the Livingstonia missions. But Laws' attitudes toward female professionals were another matter entirely. His treatment of medical missionary Jane Waterson drove her from Livingstonia after a few months. She rejected the chauvinistic attitudes women were subjected to in Laws' time. Waterson fought these barriers for years before her arrival in Africa. The story of her successful struggle in becoming a medical doctor in Britain is proof positive of her grit in confronting, and then conquering, certain societal 'norms' of her time.

"Going up that river was like traveling back to the earliest beginnings of the world, when vegetation rioted on the earth and the big trees were kings. An empty stream, a great silence, an impenetrable forest. The air was warm, thick, heavy, sluggish. The long stretches of the waterway ran on, deserted into the gloom of overshadowed distances. On silvery sandbanks hippos and alligators sunned themselves side by side. The broadening waters flowed through a mob of wooded islands. You lost your way on that river as you would in a desert and butted all day long against shoals trying to find the channel till you thought yourself bewitched and cut off for ever from everything you had known."

—Joseph Conrad, *Heart of Darkness*

Note to Reader: To minimize disrupting the story, not all misspellings and unusual abbreviations in Sutherland's journal are highlighted. The author's handwriting was difficult to decipher, as was his quirky sentence structure and unfamiliar spelling of certain words. He references objects, native plants, recreational games, etc. we simply aren't familiar with. A traveling companion exclaimed, "Polebe," during the discussion about the sunken steamboat in the Zambesi River. The reader wonders what it means (although one can imagine). Sutherland commonly employed the term "station" where I use "mission" in referencing the same thing. I use "tribal member," where Sutherland instead chose "native." Sutherland benefitted from schools students of limited economic means were able to attend. This educational system was one of the greatest achievements of the Scottish Enlightenment period in the late 18th and early 19th centuries. I hope the reader finds James Sutherland as likeable and engaging as I have over the past few years. —R. Haynes

Steamline Advertisment
for Travel to Africa

Sutherland's Transport from
Aden to Quilimane: *SS Iona*

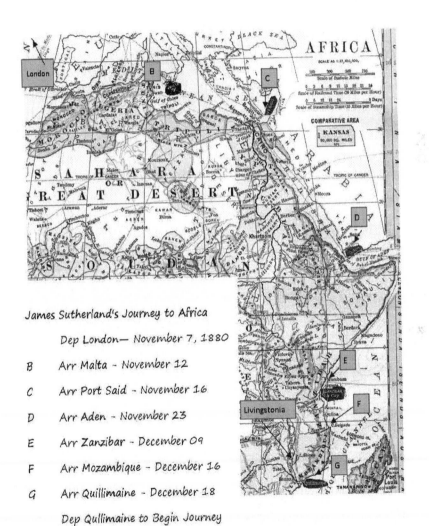

James Sutherland's Journey to Africa

Dep London— November 7, 1880

B   Arr Malta - November 12

C   Arr Port Said - November 16

D   Arr Aden - November 23

E   Arr Zanzibar - December 09

F   Arr Mozambique - December 16

G   Arr Quillimaine - December 18

Dep Qullimaine to Begin Journey
Up Zambesi River to Livingstonia
Mission Station - Dec 23, 1880

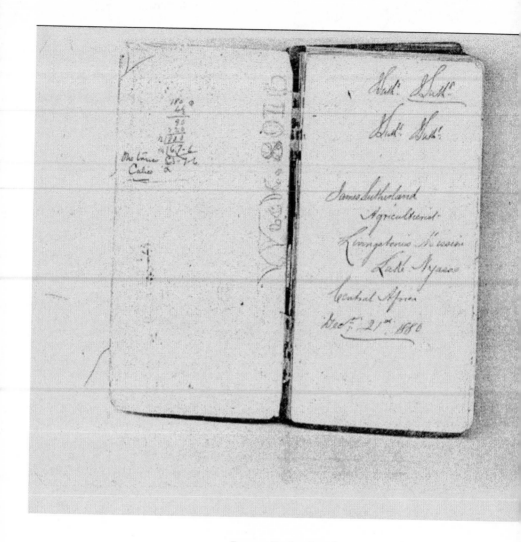

James Sutherland
Agriculturist
Livingstonia Mission
Lake Nyasa
Central Africa
Dec 21st 1880

Better Than Gold[31]

Better than grandeur, better than gold.
Than ranks' and titles a thousand-fold
Is a health body and mind at-Ease
And simple pleasures that always please
A heart that can feel for another's woes
And share its joys With a genial glow
With sympathies large enough to enfold
All men are brothers better than gold

Better than gold is the sweet-repose
Of the sons oftail when their labours close
Better than gold is the poor man's sleep
Or the balm that drop from his slumbers' deep
Bringing sleeping draughts to the dowry bed
Where luxury pillows its aching head
But—he has simple opiate deems
A shorter route to the land of dreams

Better than gold is the thinking mind
That within the realm of books can find
A treasure surpassing Australian ore

— Abram Joseph Ryan

---

[31] Sutherland opens with a poem by A.J. Ryan (1838–1886), a mid
19th century American poet. Ryan served as a Roman Catholic
chaplain with the Rebel troops during the American Civil War. He
was widely known as, "The Poet-Priest of the South."

Nov 2nd 1880 – Early January 1881

Left London, Victoria Docks by the *SS Dorinda*, Capt Withers. Arrived off Gibraltar on the evening of the Sabbath Nov. 7th and stayed till Monday morning. On Friday 12th Nov. we put into Malta for the purpose of coaling and rode at anchor for 6 hours. We had a look at the town, its principal places of interest, etc. At 4:30, we left Malta and proceeded on our further voyage to Port Said, where we put in on the morning of Tuesday 16th Nov. Port Said is an abominably filthy town of modern standing with 12,000 inhabitants. In the evening we left this port and entered the Suez Canal[32] and proceeded 6 miles and then moored for the night. During next day we went 40 miles, and at sunset—[?] up for another night—on the afternoon of Thursday eighteenth Nov. we reached Suez, where we stayed an hour to despatch and receive letters. Started for Aden, our next port of call and arrived there on the evening of Tuesday 23rd Nov. Being late

---

[32] Completed in 1869, the Suez Canal eventually came under the "direct supervision" of the British Empire in 1882. For many years into the future, England and France would squabble over control of the Canal.

we did not go ashore till the following morning. On Wednesday morning we went ashore and put up in the Hotel De Le Univers for 3 days at an expense of (1 pound 13 shillings 4 pence) each for the time being. In Aden we had to stay a week for a steamer to take us down to Quilimane. We went on the *SS Iona* on Saturday 27th and left Aden on Wednesday Dec 1st.

> **Author comment**: In the late 19th century there were two basic types of paddle steamers: the stern variety, most often utilized in open ocean transport; and side wheelers, utilized as riverboats and coastal craft because of their better maneuverability. In Aden, Sutherland embarked on *SS Iona*, a steam-screw vessel whose boiler powered a drive shaft attached to a stern screw (propeller). *Iona* was retired from service, replaced by a much larger new side-wheeler bearing the same name in 1883.

On the evening of Thursday Dec 9th we arrived at Zanzibar and on Friday 10th we went ashore and paid a visit to Dr. John Kirk, Counsel.[33] We were sorry to hear from Dr. Kirk that certain cruel treatment was carried out at Livingstonia; that he had heard from Mr. Cherryside that Mr. James Stewart introduced a flogging machine to Blantyre, that he acted as [?], that is to tramp on the toes of the natives with his hob-nailed boots, etc. On the forenoon of Saturday the 11th Capt. Bailey and myself visited the *SS Punjant*, in order that we might get some information from the missions sent out by the Church of Scotland [sponsor of Blantyre mission] to investigate the Blantyre Mission tragedy [flogging incidents]. We introduced

---

[33]   Dr. John Kirk was a medical officer, economic botanist, and former explorer-companion of David Livingstone. At the time Sutherland met him he was serving as British Counsel of Zanzibar. Like Sir Harry Johnston (he will be introduced shortly), Kirk was a major actor for Britain during the scramble. One historian today writes of Kirk: "he was a tall, taciturn Scot, the last of Livingstone's lieutenants in the field. If anyone had inherited the mantle of Livingstone it was not Stanley (as Stanley claimed), but Sir John Kirk." *The Scramble for Africa: White Man's Conquest of the Dark Continent From 1876 to 1912*, Thomas Pakenham, (Avon Books, NY, 1991), p. 286.

3

ourselves to Dr. Rankin, parish church minister of Strathearne near Coriff.[34] He gave us a few valuable hints as to our journey up the rivers. Further, he related a few incidents regarding the Livingstonia Mission. 1st that it was his opinion that the [African

---

[34] Daniel J. Rankin, was to become a celebrated explorer of the Zambesi River delta. He also became Secretary of British Protectorate of Nyasa-land under Consulate Foote, Captain, Royal Navy (RN) in 1883. Employed by the Royal Geographic Society, Rankin was recognized by the RGS for his discovery of the Chinde Bar entrance to Zambesi River from the Indian Ocean, at the time considered a significant achievement. In 1893 Rankin penned his book, *The Zambesi Basin and Nyassaland*, William Blackwood and Sons publishers, Edinburgh & London. Rankin and Sutherland took the same route up the Zambesi and Shire Rivers, like many others. Rankin's writing style and tone is oriented towards commercial publishing. Sutherland did not write assuming a large audience was looking over his shoulder. Rankin, a missionary with a medical degree, demonstrates more of an academic flair. Sutherland's voice is more personal. Their individual depictions of local scenery, wildlife, and native cultures, are vivid and informative for those wanting to know more about the region and its peoples and diverse wildlife in the Victorian colonial period. Rankin and Sutherland's writings complement each other, in many respects.

Lakes] Company was bankrupt, that he would give two pence for a share in the company.[35] Dr Rankin said further that he could get to Livingstonia, but from all accounts that he had heard, the Livingstonia Mission was planted in a very unhealthy spot, a swamp behind, a high hill in front, that there was not comfort at the mission night or day.[36] The members of

---

[35] The African Lakes Company (ALC) was formed by lay members of the Glasgow Livingstonia Committee in 1877–78, with two brothers, John and Frederick Moir, appointed as the first managers. One biographer of the early Livingstonia Mission wrote of the ALC, "it proved a considerable benefit to the natives themselves by revealing to them the blessings of trade and showing them how they could live honorably and perhaps enrich themselves in some honourable way." The PS Ilala was given to the ALC by Livingstonia Mission in 1881. The missionaries and traders plied Lake Nyasa's waters together aboard the steamer, as Sutherland notes later on in his journal. Daybreak in Livingstonia, p. 218.

[36] Scottish evangelist and anthropologist, Professor Henry Drummond visited the mission several times in the 1880s on scientific research missions. He once called the Livingstonia Mission at Cape Maclear, "one of the loveliest spots in the world." Daybreak in Livingstonia, p.59. Drummond worked closely with American evangelist Dwight L. Moody [of Moody Institute of Chicago fame], holding many revivals in Britain in the 1870s.

the mission go out under sentence of death and had it
not been for harping of the church about the
suitability of the place, as a grand spot for planting a
mission, a fact which is absurd, they might have
known a few months after they had settled that the
present site was unhealthy and now he said that they
were to shift their camp further up the country which
they might have done years ago.

Zambesi River, and its great tributary to the north, the Shire." [37] It was approximately 400 miles from the Indian Ocean to Cape Maclear by water, over 800 miles by land. Stewart sought independent financial support from Glasgow businessmen, not the Free Church, to establish Livingstonia in keeping with Livingstone's vision of the "3-Cs." Dr. Robert Laws would work to more closely integrate Livingstonia's operations with ALC.[38] A separate assessment of the economic viability of the ALC is offered by modern historian John McCracken who notes that by 1881 the Moir brothers

---

[37] Ibid, p. 27.

[38] Recent writings about ALC explain that the entity's private investments were, in the beginning, intended to commemorate David Livingstone's spiritual values, which meshed nicely with the work ethic normally associated with Victorian commerce. The ALC also chose Livingstonia because it was on the shoreline of Lake Nyasa, and the Company had a long-term commitment to the project. J. McCracken, p.61. In 1893 Daniel Rankin wrote, "this eccentric attempt to combine the hetegenuous offices of priest and trader met with little success financially and gradually devolved into a transport agency for the various local missions ... [but] it is to them we owe the roads and facilities of communication that have been so effectuated in the opening of this large region. Indeed the colony may almost be said to owe its existence to the indomitable determination of these pioneers during the critical stages of its early history."— D. Rankin, pp. 257-8.

abandoned recruiting native employment for their corporation, finding it financially unsustainable. Instead, they pursued commercial opportunities in the ivory trade.*39*

Lake Nyasa is unhealthy on its shores, that there is no trade on the Lake for the *Ilala*; a canoe could do all the work that she has got to do. It is all a sham from beginning to end. Flogging was first introduced by Mr James Stewart,[40] from thence introduced to

---

39 *Politics & Christianity in Malawi: The Impact of the Livingstonia Mission In the Northern Provence*, John McCracken. Kachere Monograph No. 8, Kachere Series, Zomba, 2008, p.76.

40 **Author comment:** James Stewart, a Scottish civil engineer who had spent time as a missionary in India, was the <u>cousin</u> of Dr. James Stewart of the Loveland mission in South Africa. Before helping erect Livingstonia II at Bandawe, Stewart surveyed 800 miles of the western shore of Lake Nyasa. Concerning the flogging of natives, a Stewart biographer wrote sympathetically that, "[native] stealing at Blantyre and Livingstonia was a serious problem ... James Stewart was a frequent victim and when his box of best clothing was purloined he determined that when a delinquent was caught he would be severely punished as a lesson to others." —*Laws of Livingstonia*, p. 134. This same source describes Mr. Stewart's character: "he was a man of high Christian character, of self-denying devotion, and of unique scientific skill

Blantyre by him, that he otherwise maltreated the natives by flogging and then rubbing salt in their wounds, that the L. [Livingstonia] people were going to slander, speaking ill of their neighbours, criticizing

---

— his gentleness, his fair dealing, and his Christian disposition speedily gained the esteem of the surrounding tribes." For an extended time there were serious jurisdictional questions at the Livingstonia missions, about where the civil authority of the Station began and ended, questions that were only finally addressed by the Foreign Services Office in London once the scramble was well underway. Was civil authority to be applied just within mission grounds and by certain mission staff only? If not, where, and to whom, and how far would the authority reach? Only after public pressure grew in England did the British government intervene with force to protect the missions in the pre-scramble period. The flogging incident received the tacit approval of the Convener [Head] of the Free Church of Scotland Foreign Missions Committee, but not the Committee (the sponsor of Livingstonia) itself. The debate about civil, political, and military jurisdiction-related issues plagued overseas Christian missions for years. The local situation was complicated by the number of European nations in Africa (in the early years nations did not generally antagonize each other in areas where multiple nations claimed interests), as well as by problems related to tribe-on-tribe competition and violence. *Laws of Livingstonia,* pp. 134–135, and *Daybreak in Livingstonia,* p. 96.

them and otherwise sarcastically referring to them and then reporting their ill conduct in letters sent home. That they were meddling and busy-bodies in other people's matters when they ought to mind their own affairs. Miss Waterson[41] stayed at Blantyre on her way from Livingstonia to the coast and was hospitably treated by Mr. & Mrs. McDonald and parted on very friendly terms, but when she reached Quillimaine she told Mr. Nunes, Counsel, that the Blantyre people were a lot of devils, on board the steamer she spoke of the Blantyre mission in the same spirit at meals, To the Mozambique Counsel she told

---

[41] Waterson was a medical doctor-missionary from Lovedale Mission in South Africa who opened a boarding school for girls there in 1867. The story of her relentless quest to become a doctor at a time when society frowned upon such pursuits is compelling. A forceful, unapologetic individual, Waterson might be considered the British Empire's Susan B. Anthony-equivalent of her day, in the field of medicine and missionary work. She published a book about her life with the Lovedale and the Lake Nyasa missions in the early 1900s, transcribing her many letters to friends and associates while stationed overseas as the main source of her writing.

the same story, and lastly, she told the same word to Dr. Kirk, Counsel at Zanzibar.

Author comment: Less than 2 months into his new career, Sutherland learns first-hand about the constant bickering between mission staff members, anticipating the often testy relations between the missionaries and tribal members, with incidents occasionally escalating to violence. Daily tensions from the poor living conditions the missionaries endured are understandable. But this rumor-mongering surely gave Sutherland pause about what he would find at Livingstonia. In his lengthy autobiography about his life in Africa in 1906, former Counsel-General in British Central Africa, Sir Harry H. Johnston, a key figure in British colonial politics in the Mozambique/Lake Nyasa region during the Scramble for Africa, singles out Universities Mission (Church of Scotland, sponsor) and Livingstonia (Free Church of Scotland, sponsor) as examples of what he calls the British African missionary's "mawkish piety and…statements which are an insidious perversion of the truth… there is an undoubted tendency on the part of the missionaries to hold and set forth the opinion

11

that no one ever did any good in Africa but themselves. That they have done more good than armies, navies, conferences, and treaties have yet done. I am prepared to admit; that they have prepared the way for the direct and just rule of European Powers, and for the extension of sound and honest commerce I have frequently asserted; but they are themselves to some extent only a passing phase, only John-the-Baptists, the forerunners of organized churches and settled social politics. It is their belief that they hold an always privileged position, that they are never to fit into their proper places in an organized European community, which causes so much the friction between them and the other European settlers."[42]

Author comment: Johnston is writing about 'propaganda' in mission reports, diaries, and other writings for public consumption. At the same time he is also tacitly acknowledging how difficult mission life was. He wants a more candid description of missionary life in

---

[42] *British Central Africa: The Territories Under British Influence North of the Zambesi*, Sir Harry H. Johnston, Methuen & Co., London, 1903, p. 192.

Victorian Africa that most accounts on the subject tended to sidestep. Contemporary Scottish historian John McCracken urges objective examinations of, "the myths and legends that attach themselves to major figures like Robert Laws ..."[43] to look past the Victorian era propaganda about Christian missionary work in China, India, and Africa. Without mincing words, McCracken points to the, "weaknesses and inaccuracies in their accounts which modern scholarship is beginning to rectify."[44] The stories of some of Sutherland's contemporaries seem fantastic, lacking the less glamorous aspects of missionary life in Africa. More than a few missionary accounts omit or downplay the inevitable frictions that arise between members living in close proximity to one another under arduous conditions.

These gentlemen, says Dr. Rankin, told him from their own lips what Miss Waterson had reported to them. What do you think of such conduct on the part of

[43] *Politics & Christianity in Malawi: The Impact of the Livingstonia Mission In the Northern Provence*, John McCracken, p.16

[44] Ibid. p.22.

your mission? It is a disgrace on the lady, says he. This is a condensed report of Rankin's statement, which he means to lay before the public at home. Because their Blantyre Mission and church have been slandered by our church and Mission, Dr. Rankin took down our names for memory sake. We could get nothing out of Dr. Rankin about the Blantyre Mission,[45] other than they were getting on well. We left Zanzibar on Sabbath 12th Dec at 6:30 am. Got along with us a present from Dr. Kent consisting of a Rifle, ammunition, and clothes to one of the Makolo Chiefs named Mashema in return for an ivory tusk which he got from the Chief. Arrived in Mozambique on Wednesday 16th Dec and stayed 24 hours. Visited

---

[45] Blantyre was named after the birthplace of David Livingstone, located near Glasgow. The map on page xvii shows the Church of Scotland's (Presbyterian) Blantyre mission's location near the Upper Shire River, not far south of the Free Church of Scotland's Livingstonia I mission on Lake Nyasa's Cape Maclear. Theological differences aside, Livingstonia and Blantyre staff interacted often, especially before Livingstone II relocated to Bandawe in 1881 soon after Sutherland's arrival.

the foot and printing establishment. Left on Thursday forenoon and arrived off Quilemane on Friday evening about 9:00 pm. The Captain in a fix, being timorous to go further. Anchored off Quilemane bar at 8:00 am, crossed the bar at 4:00 pm on Saturday and reached the town of Quilemane at 6 pm. Went ashore on Sabbath morning and proceeded to home of Vice Counsel, got instructions about leaving for Livingstonia. Lodged in a Portuguese house for the time we stay here. Hope to leave on Wednesday afternoon on the 22nd Dec. Left Quilemane on the evening of Thursday Dec 23rd 1880 at 8:00 pm on a nice clean commander's launch 24 feet by 5 ½. We have on board six tin boxes, 8 wooden ones, bag of rice, 4 large bundles. Her Majesty's mails for Blantyre and Livingstonia missions. 3 [?] of wine capable of containing 5 gallons each, one [?] of John of water, and the provisions belonging to the crew, the whole cargo weighing 2 tons. The crew consists of a skipper and cook and 6 boatmen who propel the boat by means of paddle, in all 10 souls including ourselves.

At 8:30 we stopped at the village of Numba for breakfast. We left at 10:30 am and proceeded on our journey for another hour when we moored until the tide turned. At 5:30 we proceeded on our way at a good sharp rate probably 6 knots an hour till nearly 12 midnight when we halted at the village of Verando, at the confluence of the Luwala with the Muto [?]. The morning at 9:30 am we started along with the stream. Progress much impeded by floating debris. Arrived at the village of Groomba at 6:40 pm and halted for the night—crew well worn after working hard from morning to night. Groomba at 5:40 am on Christmas morning. Beautiful morning and very warm. Halted for the night at a native village at 6:30 pm.[46] On Sabbath morning 26th Dec we

---

[46] **Author comment:** Daniel Rankin described this dramatic scene on a Christmas Day near this location 10 years later: "...stamping on our fires, our dinner, and tent with blind rage and gratuitous ferocity were two huge rhinoceros, who continued their work of vicious destruction till they had flattened out everything in camp. Unfortunately our guns were down below, and we had to remain unwilling though interested spectators until the brutes had finished

left—very early in the morning and most of the day was spent in navigating swamp. At 6:40 we halted at a native village for the night. About 5 am on Monday morning the boat was got underway and slow progress made, the boat having to be dragged for miles along the shallow river, Halted for breakfast at 9:40. At 3:30 PM on the afternoon of Monday Dec 27th we arrived at Marendinny from thence travelled [sic] to Mazaro 4 miles distant—where we stay until the *Lady Nyasa*[47] is launched and made it fit for sea in a few days.[48]

---

their performance and retired." *Zambesi Basin and Nyassaland*, D. Rankin, p.28.

[47] **Author comment:** in 1878 Livingstonia Mission I donated the *Lady Nyasa*'s sister ship *Ilala* to the African Lake Company from Glasgow. It was mostly used for steaming close to Lake Nyasa's shoreline, and up and down the Shire and Zambesi Rivers.

[48] **Author comment:** echoing other missionaries' observations about the sea-worthiness of the vessel, Jane Waterson wrote, "the *Lady Nyasa* is very leaky and unsafe and is no boat. She is just a shell. Both engineers say it was a mistake building her at Quillimane." *The Letters of Jane Elizabeth Waterson, 1866–1905*, J. E. Waterson, The Van Riebeeck Society, publisher, 1983, p.155.

Jane Elizabeth Waterson
Medical Missionary
Lovedale Mission, South Africa

Author comment: in the early 1900s medical doctor missionary Jane Elizabeth Waterson wrote extensively in her letters about the early situation at Blantyre and Livingstonia, referencing, ". . . Blantyre's incompetent foundation. While Livingstonia had begun its work in a reasonably effective manner, the Established Church Mission [at Blantyre] had been struggling. Although Henderson[49] in 1876 had chosen an excellent site for the mission, albeit inadvertently, he had neither the qualities of leadership nor the evangelical zeal to carry out pioneer missionary work, a fact which he recognized. He told [Dr] James Stewart on December 1876, 'I am not **able**, neither am I **fitted** to carry on the work [here] ... with assistants of poor caliber and without clear instructions from the home committee, the station rapidly became demoralised [sic] and in December 1876 Henderson appealed to Livingstonia for help. Reluctantly [Dr.] Stewart

---

[49] **Author comment:** Henry Henderson was the son of a Scottish parish minister in Kinclaven, Scotland. He served both as the business manager at Blantyre and principal lay leader for a time. Henderson was one of the early founders of that mission.

and Laws agreed and Stewart went to Blantyre where he was detained for over 3 months … In the absence of any clergy the atmosphere at the Station had become thoroughly secularized, while the artisans had gained increasing and unsuitable influence. Not only did they have numbers of workmen under their charge, but some had acquired substantial tracts of territory from local chiefs…the artisans taking the law literally into their own hands, on one occasion brutally executing a man. When they viciously whipped an innocent man to death and [Blantyre artisan] Macklin tried to cover it up by declaring he had a heart defect it was clear things were out of hand…Livingstonia did not escape the scandal unscathed…no more than Blantyre could it avoid the need occasionally to discipline offenders amongst the dependents who settled the Station…It was not the principle of inflicting punishment which was at issue but its nature and degree of severity. In addition there was the question of the extent to which Livingstonia condoned the atrocities at Blantyre, turning a blind eye there…some of the artisans were no better quality than those at Blantyre. Amongst the worst was the illiterate Thomas Crooks who assaulted another artisan in a drunken temper

and was dismissed because of his brutal
treatment of the Africans in his charge."[50]

Wednesday, 5th January

Usually rise between 6 and seven o'clock.
Received cup of coffee. Breakfast at 11 am.
After breakfast we had a few rounds of Rifle
shooting. Target being a bottle on an ant hill
100 yards distant. I fired two shots for the first
time in my life and knocked down some leaves
from a mangoe [sic] tree instead of shooting
even the ant hill. The sun has been dreadfully
hot—so much so as to lay the Carpenter down
with fever, wrought some at the *PS Lady Nyasa*
in the carpenter business. Dinner at 7 pm.
Retired to rest at 9:30.

---

[50] *The Letters of Jane Elizabeth Waterson, 1866–1905*, J. E.
Waterson, The Van Riebeeck Society, publisher, 1983, pp. 141–
142.

Thursday 6th January 1881

Rose at 5:30 and went down to the steamer and wrought a little at my usual recreation. At 12 Noon the Carpenter Engineers halted working for a couple of hours until it got cool. At 7 pm work was finished for a day. We got the cabin roof on the steamer in the afternoon. Retired to rest at 10 pm.

Friday January 7th Mazaro

Rose at 7:30 and after partaking of a cup of coffee went down to the steamer. Sad night— with rats scouring about the house. Several hyenas and a leopard visited the square during the night but no damage was done. The goats kept bleating for a long while, in the afternoon rain fell and continued till late. At 8 pm we have to leave Ghaistangs house and make our abode in the steamer. We, Mr. McIlvaine, Capt. Fairley [Captain of the vessel], and myself therefore got our beds conveyed from the house to P.S. by the boys. While we were flitting the rain was falling and the moon in consequence was observed. By 9 PM the boxes were laid down across the cabin and my bed was spread on them. About 10 o'clock turned in.

> **Author comment**: One visitor to Mazaro wrote: "Mazaro proved to be a wretched little settlement with a meagre [sic] population living in terror of lions and native raiders."
> *Laws of Livingstonia*, W.P. Livingstone, p 55.

Saturday January 8th

Rose at 6 AM after spending a rare night continuous sleeping [unintelligible] expense of

Jack Cameron who lay on the floor beside us. Now and again we heard the cry of the hyena and a visit from a leopard or some other beast of the jungle keeping us awake during the whole night— In spite of nets we could not prevent the horrible mosquitoes from singing and praying [sic] upon us. They got in under the curtain, it was with much difficulty that we could rid of them. However daylight came at last and our minds and bodies were [unintelligible]. There is a nice breeze blowing down the line. Capt Fairley and Mr. Henderson are away today on a visit to an opium grower Alberto D'Iaiva Repose. I have to ride from Mazaro to Mopea. Prepare for bed at 9 PM.

Sabbath January 9th 1881

Rose about 7 am and read some. The day is dull and dreary here, no church service. The day is beautiful and a strong breeze was blowing down the river most of the day. In the afternoon Mr. McIlvaine and I had a walk to Maruras, the residence of Sehnor Leopold D'Azevedo, about 2 miles from Mazaro. Our road lay through a dense jungle of long grass towering many feet above our heads. Mr. D'Azevedo received us kindly. Here we stayed for an hour. Saw about 20 head of nice, fat oxen and cows. Mr. D'Azevedo suffers a great deal from the attacks of leopards on his herd. He showed us the foot tracks of a leopard in a brick which was laid in the sun today. Returned to Mazaro after being absent about two hours and a half. In the evening we returned to the cabin of the *Lady Nyasa* and went early to bed.

Monday January 10th Mazaro

Managed to get astir at 6 am much refreshed. Wrought some during the day in the way of painting and puttying the seams in the deck. The day was first rate for working, a steady breeze was blowing steadily down the river the most of the day. After duske [sic] we lit the candle in the cabin and wrote a few words. In the morning and evening crowds of natives came to the rivers edge for washing and bathing purposes. The female sex are somewhat indecent. Retire about 10 PM.

Tuesday January 11th Mazaro

Rose about 6 AM. The floor of the *Lady Nyasa* submerged in water. The carpenters with the assistance of Captain Fairley and James Sutherland convened together and stated their opinions,

26

regarding the wholesale calamity that had befallen the *Lady Nyasa*. On the motion of Mr. Sutherland, Mr. Henderson was called upon to preside, seconded by Mr. Ramsay, Engineer. Mr. Henderson said that a very sad and unexpected calamity had befallen the *Lady Nyasa* today. Such an event was never anticipated by any of us.[51]

---

[51] **Author comment:** from Daniel Rankin's book chronicling his travels on the Zambesi and Shire Rivers aboard the *PS Lady Nyasa* a decade after James Sutherland's trip: "one-half of [the stern area], we were informed, was set apart for bailing purposes, to keep the steamer afloat." —*The Zambesi Basin and Nysassaland*, Rankin, p. 6. *Nyasa* continued to have watertight integrity problems. As noted earlier, the practice of disassembling and reassembling these small river steamers at the impassable points of waterways—the Murchison cataracts on the Shire River, named after Royal Geographic Society (RGS) President Roderick Murchison by David Livingstone, necessitated a 65 mile portage with long lines of natives carrying the steamer, its engineering plant and her cargo around the cataracts—was undoubtedly the source of the leaks on *Lady Nyasa* and other vessels of her kind.

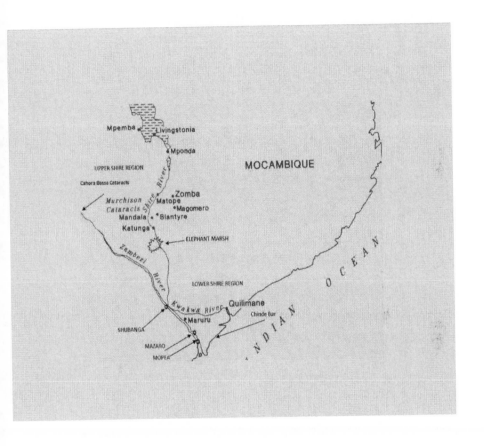

With the flooding of the *Lady Nyasa*, the travelers were stranded near Mazaro. This map shows landmarks Sutherland's group passed over the next month.

Author comment: The following entry was lined out on a page of the journal, but it is still legible. It is not clear whether these are Sutherland's words or those of another passenger, nor why they were left readable.

I am sure Gentlemen what you will all concur with me that in the workman at the Lady Nyasa performed our work as far as it was in our power, and seeing now that our labours have been in vain we cannot but feel sorry at what happened today. My candid opinion is that the work should never have been for the fact it seemed inevitable that when the sheathing was laid on the swelling of the wood would exert too great a pressure on the bolts so as to make them give way. Such has been the case today. And we all regret the misfortune which was never expected but on the other hand entertained very high hopes about the travails and the voyage to Mtebe Within these few remarks I conclude.

[CONVERSATION BETWEEN THE TRAVELERS]:

Mr. Ramsay: Well Gentlemen seeing that this great calamity has befallen us today what would you propose as the best thing to do in the circumstances, any of you has got a long head [sic].

Mr. Fairley replied by saying under the circumstances I propose that no more be done to the steamer till after you give your report to your masters at Blantyre.

Mr. Ramsay: unless that the boiler and engines be taken out.

Mr. Henderson seconded Mr. Fairley's motion.

Mr. Fairley then proposed that Mr. McIllvaine give his opinion as it is in his department the work has failed.

Mr. McIllvaine on sitting said: As you have all called it a calamity it is no doubt a great calamity that has overtaken the *Lady Nyasa*. For my own part I could nothing to that steamer. I wrought as faithfully at the work as I possibly could on the sheathing work. I never expected, nor could for one moment conjecture such an event that has taken

30

place today. The *Lady Nyasa* has not been launched a week, and the first-part of the week nothing so serious could be Entertained about the leaking of the ship. The only thing that I can say is that several bolts sprung today one or two in the cabin and a like number in the Engine room, some of which could let in your little fringes and not— Gentlemen I have nothing more to say, unless I go in for a repetition of the same thing.

Mr. Fairley: Mr. Ramsay you have something to say have you not?

Mr. Ramsay: All that I have to say is Polebe. [??]

Mr. Fairley: We don't want a native interpretation of what you have to say.

Mr. Ramsay: I think the best thing we can do is let the steamer alone until the water rises and then pull her up on the dry ground and let her lie there.

Mr. Fairley: How long will that be?

Mr. Ramsay: It may be very soon if there is plenty of rain in the Zambesi. It may be a week or it may be months.[52]

Mr. Fairley: There is one thing I can say that since I came here what I saw of the vessel. She was in good working order, both the Carpenting and Engineering work and little did I think this day that she was to burst and upset the whole work. The ship in my opinion is a total wreck and too [sic] put more money out on repairing her is to throw it

---

[52] **Author comment**: While Daniel Rankin successfully retraced Sutherland's journey up river 10 years later, the silting of the Shire River in the 1890s was making it more and more impassable. Successful transport up river relied upon sufficient levels of rain runoff in the smaller tributaries feeding major rivers like the Shire. Periodic droughts were part of the climate cycles in the area, impacting both agriculture and transportation systems, until the arrival of additional railroad lines in and around British Central Africa, and in many other parts of the continent, in the coming decades rendered the river transport system less important than before. The Congo and Nile Rivers remain major transportation systems today (the Nile River is also a critical agricultural lifeline for Egypt).

into the Zambesi and I think one of you should go to Blantyre and report your case to your headmen or whoever it may be.

Mr. McIllvaine: I for my part will do no more work at the steamer.

Mr. Sutherland: I suppose you will be all willing to go.

Mr. Ramsay: I don't know that—Mr. Henderson ought to go and Mr. McIllvaine ought to go and represent the case. Can we all go Mr. Henderson.

Mr. Henderson: No.

Mr. Fairley: Well you two go. Mr. Henderson and Mr. McIllvaine and represent your case to your masters.

Mr. McIllvaine said he had no objection and would second Mr. Fairley's motion.

Mr. Fairley: The wood must have been green.

Mr. McIllvaine: The wood was not green, but it was too great a strain on the bolts that caused the misfortune.

33

Mr. Ramsay thought that after the vessel was in the water for a day or two the wood swell. Mr. Ramsay said further Take out the engines and boiler and you two go to Blantyre and see the Moirs[53] and leave me here. This ended the consultation and the motions put to the meeting were adopted and unanimously carried. We have no alternative now but to go to Mtebe in canoes we accordingly sent a note over to Sehnor Rapaso asking him if could favor us with two boats for our journey. The note was sent to his house 8 miles distant by two of the boys who returned about eight PM with an answer that he was sorry for the unlucky *Lady Nyasa*, and that he would try and get a boat and some a boat and some Kafir[54] canoes for our baggage and then we arrange for the men for the boats.

---

53 John and Frederick Moir of Glasgow, first managers of African Lakes Company on Lake Nyasa.

54 **Author comment**: in the Victorian era Portuguese explorers used "Kafir" as part of their vernacular, before the term was adopted more widely. Originally derived from Arabic—meaning infidel—in referring to black non-Muslims when they worked with slave traders along the coast of East Africa, the term was later adopted by missionaries and other Europeans during the colonial period, it was thought, in a 'less derogatory way.'

34

January 12ᵗʰ 1881 Mazaro

Spent all this day wearily, the most wearisome day since came to Mazaro. The time hung very heavily on my hand. Made some arrangements about our departure from this place. Capt Fairley obtained Mashela [Chief Mashela of the _____ tribe] to carry him to Mopea on Thursday morning to arrange with Sehnor Raposo about boats. Henderson Engineer laid down with boils and Ramsay Engineer slight fever. The *Lady Nyasa* sank in 3 feet of water. Nothing done today in the way of taking separate portions of the steamer.

January 13ᵗʰ Mazaro

Nothing of any importance transpired today. Merely walked about the place. Had a look of the *Lady Nyasa* as usual. The boys were set on to bail her out for the purpose of getting the boiler out. It took half a dozen to keep up with the in-flow, they however mastered it—so that the inlets could be easily sealed. Did not get the boiler as no men could be got to assist us. As soon as the bailing stopped the steamer sank again. Visited Mazaro village in the afternoon for the purpose of getting men to convey us to Mtebe. Witnessed the woman dancing, one danced at the time and a great many other sat-round, they sang and clapped their hands. The men sat idly by doing nothing. Successful in getting men. Mr. Fairley arranged about boats and provisions with Sehnor Raposo. Boats are to be carried here tomorrow morning.

January 14th 1881 Mazaro

Expected boats this morning but did not come, therefore we are delayed in starting on our journey. We must put up with such disappointments here as they are quite common in Africa. Got the boiler out of the steamer *Lady Nyasa* today and landed it safely on the shore. Time hanging heavily on our hands now since the wreck of the *Lady Nyasa*. Had a game with the boys in the evening with the bright rays of the moon. The boys enjoyed Puss in the Corner very much. Prepared for bed between nine and ten PM.

January 15th Mazaro

Another weary day spent in waiting for boats, and did not come to relieve our minds we sent a letter to Sehnor Raposo regarding them. His answer stated that the boats were sent away this morning and would be here today. In the Evening we got another letter saying that he sent one boat and 3 canoes. The bearer told us that the boats would be down on Sabbath morning. We cannot get away from Mazaro until Monday now seeing that the boats did not come in time. Capt Fairley cut my hair today and made a good job of it for the first time, very bright moonlight.

Had a good walk in the square under her bright beams.

January 16th Mazaro

Spent quieter day than expected. One boat came this morning. Mr. Fairley received a note of Sehnor Raposo today with the account for the provisions which amounted to L 8 [pounds]-6 [shillings] – 9 [pence] all allowing 6 L for the boat. Hope to get away soon, however we don't know exactly we have been so much disappointed in point of time that we must exercise our patience as the African takes his time in all his engagements. Enjoyed myself in reading South African Missions by C.H. Malan and finished it.[55] Retired to rest shortly after 9 PM.

---

[55] **Author comment**: Captain C.H. Malan served in the British Infantry 7th Fusiliers and was severely wounded in four places during the Crimean War. Malan was deeply religious, involved in a number of churches and missionary projects in the years that

January 17th Mazaro

Greatly annoyed today with the natives. They would not take the calico that was here because of its inferior quality. [**Author note**: calico was the local currency used to pay tribal members] They would not bargain to go to Blantyre and be paid there because they were cheated there before by getting inferior calico, no argument of ours would induce them to comply with our request—so they went away. We were now in a fix. Mr. Henderson went to Leopold Asevedo and got a few pieces from him which would enable us to pay for the boatmen of the boat and of the canoe. Each man receiving 8 fathoms for going to Mtebe and 30 fathoms for the use of the canoe. Had a two miles walk today for the purpose of cutting wood for the houses[56] on the boat. With the assistance of Mr. Jack

---

followed. He published several popular books about his adventures.

[56] **Author comment**: Probably a reference to pilot houses. Steering wheels were most frequently located in the pilot houses, and, depending on the size of the vessel and number of passengers

Camerone, Mashali Martini, and Mr. McIllvaine we managed to raise several spars from the river mud at present day. Retired to rest with hope of getting away tomorrow.

January 18th Mazaro

Still in Mazaro. How trying to our patience being so long delayed. It's best to keep calm and allow the Africans to perform their work in their own way. The boatmen came early this morn and prepared the houses for the canoes. Afterwards they went to their respective villages to buy food and necessities for the start early on the following morning. The distance we have to go to Mtebe is said to be 200 miles. Made preparations by packing up our boxes and other small things which served to beguile the weary hours of the day. Mr. Ramsay down with fever the whole day. The

---

embarked, pilot houses were sometimes used as temporary shelters.

mosquitoes gained the mastery over us tonight at the dinner table. We therefore had to be smart about it. Got a fire started in the house which alleviated our misery caused by these torments. Retire to rest after customary preparations intending well to be up with the men on the following morning.

> **Author comment**: a graphic excerpt from Daniel Rankin's book described an ordinary evening meal in the area Sutherland was passing through at this point: "... We were besieged by flying cockroaches, ants, bugs, moths, earwigs, mosquitoes, and several other varieties of the same family ... our dinner consisted of two fowls [cuckoo birds] whose dimensions would have insulted an ordinary English bantam. They were to be divided among six hungry people. A large plate of boiled rice and two or three captains' biscuits looked more sustaining if not inviting; but with the quantity of the insects seasoning each dish we could find no fault, and they certainly went a great way to satisfy our inner cravings. It was useless theming [sic] out of the food in which they swarmed, so we were obliged to eat them with our eyes shut and

susceptibles stifled. [sic] A tin of weak tea
finished our meal."
—*The Zambesi Basin and Nyassaland*,
D. Rankin, pp. 9 – 10.

January 19th Mazaro

Rose with the sun after spending a queer night—the
Eato [tribe?] kept up a series of quadrilles all the night
so much so that I had to get up and make a clearance.
I so far succeeded but in the moment silence was
restored; the same hub-bub was kept going all the
long hours of the night—Discovered on the hearth
some traces of fire which arrested Mr. McIllvaine
eliciting from him a reply, to my information by
asking if the house was on fire again. Mr. McIllvaine
at once sprang to his feet to make sure to and to his
satisfaction found that it was only the fading embers
of the previous night that had revised a little and shot
a glare around. Sadly we missed the presence of Jack
Cameron (he being sent away to Mopea with a [?] the

previous night) for his presence on the floor would lessen the caliber of the Kodietha [?] tribe. The boatmen came soon and we at once began to flit from the house we rented for 3 weeks (minus 3 days in the ill-fated *Lady Nyasa*'s cabin) to our boats. By 10 AM all the boxes were stowed away in the boat and canoes and at half-past eleven we were in our places in the boat.

Grave of Mrs. Mary Livingstone at Shupanga on the Zambesi River

The start was at once made and the boat—leading away, followed in the rear by Mr. McIllvaine canoe and Mr. Henderson's. The boat kept the first during the first run til it came to Chinpanga ['Shupanga' on certain maps] village at 4:00 in the alongside of us. We stayed at this village in the night and enjoyed ourselves admirably. On the opposite side of the river right in front of us Chinpanga house stands. Some yards to the East there is a large Baobab tree 78 feet in circumfrence [sic] and a few yards from where it lies the remains of Mrs. Livingstone. Away in the north Mr. Henderson shows us the Morambala range mountains and further away the towering peak of Mt. Clarendon. In a soon time it was dark and the best place for us to go too [sic] was our beds in our respective boats. After 9 PM I turned in but not to sleep.

Author comment: a revealing story related to Dr. Laws taking Mr. James Stewart to Shupanga on a brief visit to Mrs. Livingstone's gravesite: Mr. Stewart was said to remark to Dr. Laws, "A queer country this is, where the only things of

interest you have to show me are the graves," to
which Laws reportedly responded, "Yes, but
they are milestones of Christianity to the regions
beyond."

Daybreak in Livingstonia, J.W. Jack, p. 136

January 20th Zambesi

Rose with the first streaks of daylight. Orders were
given for coffee to be made ready. Spent a miserable
night for sleep but heartily enjoyed myself for all of
that. The mosquitoes kept up a dreadful singing and
worst of all they bit us without mercy, our limbs
being spotted over with their cruel bites. I fell asleep
midnight and snored till morning. We left Chinpanga
at half six a.m. The morning was extremely fine and
we got along gaily. We had the start of our
companions this morning again but once or twice the
current got the better of us and carried us backwards
a few yards, thus enabling the canoes to get ahead.
However, our crew wrought faithfully and by the
time that we halted for breakfast the boat was again

45

ahead of the others. The boat and canoes were dragged long distances by means of ropes, part of the crew going on the bank and shimmed along chanting their boat strains with joyful glee. At 10:30 we stopped at the village of Ramou for breakfast, Mr. Fairley superintended the cooking department, whom much praise is due for interesting himself so much in this important office, not forgetting to pay tribute to Mr. McIllvaine. At 1 PM we proceeded on our way after spending 2 hours and a half at Ramou. The boatmen wrought with a will and pushed the boat on a good speed considering the very strong current against them. In the afternoon a very unlucky occurrence happened, the rope by which the men pulled the boat snapped while turning round a corner in the bank and meeting an unusually strong current. The headman seeing the mishap sprang on a proceeding cliff in the bank and holding on by the part of the rope attached to the boat—kept it at a stand-still until the rope was again spliced. We mounted up on the bank glad to get our feet on terra

[sic] firma and walked for a mile, the boat being dragged behind. We again got into the boat and pulled along till 5 o'clock when we halted at the village of [?] for the night.

> **Author comment**: scenes from Lower Shire region described here: "... hippopotami crowded the placide [sic] backwaters and lagoons, appearing and disappearing, and gambolling [sic] as lightly and easily as a brood of wild duck; crocodiles swarmed on the sandbanks, slithering quietly into the river as the sound of the steamer reached them; large fish shot up from the water; crowned cranes, flamingoes, [sic] pelicans, herons, and kingfishers stood unconcernedly as the vessel passed or rose heavily and flew off with slow and stately movement; flocks of smaller birds, brilliant in colour [sic]and swift of wing, flashed up from the depths of the reeds and jungle and as quickly disappeared. The plains were alive with game; herds of elephants and buffalo roamed with vision, wild hog and antelope browsed in profusion; at night

lions, leopards and elephants held the land in possession. Snakes were numerous."[57]

THE NYASA HIPPOPOTAMUS

57   *Laws of Livingstonia*, W.P. Livingstone, p. 58.

January 21ˢᵗ Zambesi

Rose at 5 am and by 6:20 we were all underway. The morning was very lovely and the scenery very good. Passing through Chinpanga country the size of it as large as three of the largest English counties for which it was rented by a Portuguese at L 100 a year.

> **Author comment:** The surrounding territory was first settled by the Portuguese, who later unsuccessfully laid claim to the territory at the Berlin Conference in 1884. Appendix V offers two very different interpretations on who was entitled to claim ownership of this part of Africa. British missionary writings reported of the continuing slave trade at the time: "it went on increasing under Arab and Portuguese agents, who were generally heartless villains."
> *Daybreak in Livingstonia,* J.W. Jack, p. 193

Halted near the [?] and never slept a wink more that night—Rose at 4 am and got upon the bank butt [sic] horrible scotch greys were attacking me with unabated fury. Left this village at 8 am it being thought advisable to get as fast as possible out—of the

Marambala marsh. Our course for the day lay along Marambala range of mountains, one dense marsh. About mid-day we stopped for breakfast at a small village. Ascended the hill a few yards along with Mr. Henderson and sat under the shade of a tree. Indian corn grew on the sides of the mountain. Trees of all kinds adorned the sides of the mountain some standing forth on its summits. Banana groves, sugar cane etc etc. grew wild. Large masses of indigenous rocks projected at different altitudes. The cool air where we eat was very refreshing, how different from the miasma which we inhaled in every breath during the travelling. [sic] Visited a nice cool stream flowing as clear as crystal from the mountain sides. Bathed our hot feet and brows, and drank long draughts of its mineral waters. Felt much invigorated after the wash. While we were staying here Mr. Fairley felt ill and during the afternoon he got worse. Continued on our way through the swamp and by 6:30 halted for the night along a bank, which allowed of cooking space. At its best it was Zambesi custom house for breakfast. Left at 12:30 and proceeded on our way, entering into Lower Shire about 2 PM. The afternoon has been very fine and we enjoyed ourselves splendidly. Reached the village of Shamo at 5 PM. At a little distance from this village we saw a large hippopotamus snuffing and snorting in the water. It appears Mr. Fairley suddenly fell ill without warning, which was not uncommon. Illnesses come on very rapidly in Africa, on occasion striking the victim dead.

January 22nd R. Shire [Shire River]

Spent a most miserable night. From one I never slept, being bitten by cruel Nyala insects and mosquitoes. At 3:30 AM I was compelled to rise and put on my clothes. I then went ashore and lit a fire which relieved from the inatara [?] but—the mosquitoes in countless numbers were like to tear the life out of me. The coffee was soon made ready by six AM we were away the morning was again fine and everything around us attracted our admiration. Halted at 11 am for breakfast on the right bank of the Shire. Left at 1:30 pm a good repast of ____ [?] and pancakes made by Mr. McIllvaine. The Marambala mountains are right ahead of us, a magnificent sight all covered with rich vendura, presenting at certain elevations large masses of rock. Made a good journey today. Sailed about 9 hours. Halted at the village Labulla for the evening.

January 23rd R. Shire

Spent a most miserable night being afflicted with the two most grievous plagues which travellers [sic] in Africa are subjected: a miserable spot, millions of Nyala ants lined the banks and mosquitoes buzzed on every hand. Went to bed after having a cup of tea and some biscuits, the very idea of cooking more was dispelled with the many inconveniences around.

January 24th R. Shire

Left at 6:30 am. Still in the marsh. Another days sailing before we get out of it. The day is extremely hot. By 11:30 the boats pushed in through the marsh where there is a landing place. Here we have breakfast and further we have decided to stay in this unhealthy bog until tomorrow morning. Had we left this afternoon no bank would be got to tonight, this would necessitate the men to rest in the canoes, which would deny them sleep. Therefore we propose to start early to-morrow morning so as to reach a village by night. Took a dose of quinine today on account of the unhealthy marsh in which we are situated. Feel quite well but oh the heat is oppressive.

> **Author comment:** Among numerous other maladies, David Livingstone suffered from malaria in Africa, relying on a quinine solution he created to quell the symptoms of the disease. Some victims of the disease used it as a prophylactic, a preventive drug to stave off disease, if sufficient quantities were available. Others used quinine only when ailments or symptoms appeared.

As noted elsewhere in this book, the use of quinine and steamboats in Africa were used to their advantage by missionaries and colonists. Modern weapons, the telegraph, improvements in western medicine in general, and the building of more railroads as the 19th century ended also contributed to the successes of the imperial powers during the Scramble for Africa.

January 25th R. Shire

Spent a first rate night, slept as sound as a top. Heavy showers of rain fell during the night, some of which came through the roof of our craft—and fell right upon our faces, however did not waken me for a deep sleep had taken hold of me owing to my sleep being much broken for a few nights previous by the mosquitoes. The post-night however the mosquitoes were cheated because on the previous day I sewed up all the holes in my mosquitoe [sic] curtain. We spent 19 hours in the marsh, on all hands the marsh created a stinking smell which was anything but favourable to our respiratory organs. The boatmen tell us before we went to bed the night before that they intended to start on the journey when the moon rose about 2 am. They, however, did not fulfill their promises through some paltry excuse and the sun was nearly above the horizon before they got underway. About 6 am we were away at a good rate. The day was nice and cool after the rains, a steady breeze ransomed us action and sent us along at a good rate. The headman hoisted a big sail which he made from a piece of waste awning which was for a little use, the floating miasma carried by the wind was very disagreeable to the nasal organs. By 5 in the afternoon we reached a bank after we had finished the Marambala Marsh. Here we stayed for the night and got our food cooked decently. At Midday we drew the boats along the right side of the river and rested for an hour. We continued to start a fire in a clog [?] spot at the prow of the boat and boiled the kettle for tea. We there partook of a good diet of prescoves [?]. Just when we stopped the Blantyre mail camp joined us and the mails were opened when letters were found for Mr.'s McIllvaine and Henderson. We got our limited sugar supplies also in one aside. News was brought that John Moir's house at Blantyre had fallen. Capt. Fairley had a very sore time of it today with bile and fever. When the evening came he became quieter after getting a passage in his bowels.

Author comment: the author's reference to "miasma" could be his witnessing great clouds of mosquitoes rising in the early morning hours from low-lying water or swamps, creating a sense of a cloud or noxious vapor being released. In her *Little House* series, American pioneer author Laura Ingalls Wilder echoes the prevailing belief on the western frontier in the late 1800s that breathing "bad night air" caused malaria-like illnesses. We now know mosquitoes are a major source of malaria and other deadly jungle illnesses.

January 26ᵗʰ R. Shire

Rose this morning with daylight after enjoying a sound sleep. After coffee we started on our way about 6 am. The morning was as beautiful and warm which makes the travelling [sic] Enjoyable. Both sides of the River are growing rank with Bamboo and reeds. Now and again we got a sight of Banana trees. At 10:30 am we stop on the right bank of the River for breakfast. After a pleasant repast we started on our way again at 15 minutes to one PM. The wind blew softly astern and by aid of a small sail we got on gaily. I enjoyed a few minutes at paddle immensely, but would not like to spend a whole day at it—under such a stifling heat. The natives can endure a great amount of heat and fatigue. Today they have wrought hard for 9 hours. Nothing of any note has happened today. On on on [sic] through a marshy country with no variation in the scenery. Arrived tonight at one of the village on the Shire at 5:15 PM nearly half an hour before Mr.

Henderson's canoe came alongside. Here we stay for the night.

January 27th '81 R. Shire

Before we went to bed on the previous night an hippopotamus [sic] kept up an awful snuffing on the opposite side of the river from us. He kept his own quarter however and did not pay us a visit during the night, went off to sleep regardless of his presence and slept soundly till daylight—next morning. The routine of our days journey is as follows, we all started. In about an hour the men called at a village in quest of food but were not successful further than getting a few unripe bananas. Here we purchased four fowls for one yard of calico. The boats were

ON MLANJE MOUNTAIN

Mountain scene from
Shire River

again pushed off and after another half hour vigorous paddling the boatmen called at a second village we bought 1 ½ dozen eggs for another yard of calico. Before we proceeded further the breakfast was cooked. Mr. Henderson baked a few pancakes and fired them on the frying pan. I being asked to place the pan on the fire got—hold of it by the handle and shaking some dust out of it the handle snapped and I remained in possession of the handle when the unfortunate pan fell bang to the ground. I looked blanke [sic] at the event—seeing there was no chance in getting the separate pieces put together again on the Shire. However we did not lose our pancakes, but got them nicely fired on the handle—less frying pan and they tasted nicely with a nice cup of good tea. After spending 2 hours here we set off again at full-speed. In a few minutes we overtook the two canoes that were ahead of us and without much ado passed them and soon left behind. The boatmen sang and wrought—with a will so as to keep up their good name as being leaders in the journey. The day is cloudy and dull, yet fine for travelling. [sic] To the left of us a range of mountains extending many miles in the same direction as the Shire. On the night we can see nothing but the tall grass interspersed with many kinds of fruit trees. The banana being the most conspicuous. We pass by many, many villages with their meager inhabitants, some of whom come to the river's edge to salute us being attracted by the loud alterations of the paddlers as they shout their native boat songs. After stopping at one of the villages on the left bank of the river, until the boatmen had procurred [sic] some wood, we continued on our way before we had come to a suitable place to stay for the night had enveloped us. By working on till darkness set in we made up for the time we lost during the day in searching for food. About 9 PM we enjoyed a very hearty dinner and supper combined. It generally takes two hours before a diet is cooked and eaten so

H.M.S. HERALD, CHIROMO.

Two sketches of village of Chiromo on River Shire

CHIROMO, SHIRÉ RIVER.

this accounts for the very late meal. Capt. Fairley is rather better tonight and has partaken of some fowl soup. We retired to our beds about 10 PM.

January 28th '81 R. Shire

After coffee this morning we proceeded on our way. At times the sun broke through the clouds and shone beautifully on the hills which sloped away from the right bank of the River. In the morning I enjoyed the reading of Livingstone's *First Expedition to Africa,* some of his illustrations being verified every day in our journey. Halted at 10 am for breakfast at the village of Namula. A favourable breeze sprang up and the headman hoisted a piece of canvas for a lug sail which carried us on gracefully. Heavy dark clouds gathered round and the thunder rolled which foreboded a storm of rain at 3 PM. The boats arrived at Mpassaj village where we intended to put up for the night as there are no villages nearer than a day's journey from here. The scenery around us is very enchanting, vast forests clothed in rich vendure spread out for miles on all hands. What extensive fields for enterprising farmers. In the soil there are rich stores of fortifying matters which would yield almost all kinds of produce without manure for many years to come and still few avail themselves of its prolific soils. When shall this vast continent be reclaimed and the millions of people it is capable of sustaining populate its districts. Millions of square miles of almost inexhaustible soil is lying in a state of wild confusion, the very richness of its nature causes the very ground to stink with malaria. How is this to be counteracted? Might I not mention wholesale immigration from our populated countries such as Ireland, need I say Britain at large. In a short time the dinner was cooked but before we were finished eating a severe thunderstorm came on and we were forced to beat a retreat to one of the huts carrying with the remains of our dinner.

Author comment: contemporary African historian A. Adu Boahen writes: "the main social condition contributing to the rise of the new imperialism was the need to acquire colonies where the surplus labor produced by the industrial capitalist system as well as the large numbers of the unemployed could be settled without losing their nationality or severing their links with their mother country. It was partly to undertake such colonization that a number of colonization societies emerged in Europe."[58] While Sutherland's observation and Boahen's point about surplus populations in European urban centers creating excess labor conditions are separated by over 125 years of history, they are remarkably similar.

January 29th '81 R. Shire

Slept very soundly through the past night. The previous night seemed to dampen my feelings regarding a sound sleep owing to the heavy rain that

---

[58] *African Perspectives On Colonialism*, Boahen, A., p. 31.

fell after each successive thunderclap. The rain came through the roof over Mr. Fairley's head and made his position anything but agreeable. However after the boys collected a few Mfumba (or mats) and placed them over the leaky parts it rendered our cribs more comfortable. Mr. McIllvaine & Henderson abadoned [sic] their causes and betooke themselves to one of the village huts and spent the night. They, however, escaped the rain but they were not proof to the rats which scound [sic] about during the still hours. These rodents I am told by Mr. Fairley kept up communication between the shore and the boats and went through some of their Quadrilles on the roof of our cabin not a very pleasant proceeding in the estimate of a sleepless person. Fortunately they did not come into the interior of our dwelling and disturb the sweet slumbers of its inmates. After partaking of a cup of coffee and some biscuits, we started on our way. Heavy clouds still hung overhead, but it was evident from breaks in them that the sun would gain the mastery ere long, and send forth his genial rays to brighten up the face of nature which had become drooping through the supersaturated state of the ground. My own spirits were somewhat languid and drooping as well from the same cause but the appearance of the glowing sun from behind the scattering clouds soon dispelled all dull thoughts and replaced them with more elevating ones when I gazed upon the distant hills which were twisted in many and varied colors. As we jogged along at snails pace I lay lounging and at the same time read with sage delight D. Livingstone's *First Expedition to Africa*. At 10:30 the boats came to a halt at a high bank and the breakfast was got underway. After three hours stay here we again proceeded on our journey. The boatmen were reduced to great strains for want of food except some beans, their grains being all done, and the villages by the way could not dispose of any owing to recent wars which kept the natives from cultivating their soil. The beans are not at all relished by them, inducing as they say, "pains in the stomach." The afternoon was bright and fair, the sun shone brightly and gave forth an intense heat. Under the rays of the setting sun the landscape is charming. The broad waters of the Shire as it glides gently along is in itself a picture of beauty and all is surroundings invoke within me feeling of admiration and praise to Him who has clothed nature with such smiling scenes. In the course of the afternoon I saw a huge hippopotamus at the opposite side of the River splashing about in the water with loud snuffing and after inhaling a fresh draught of air disappeared again to renew his exploration at the bottom of the stream. We stopped at the right bank of the R. for the night.

January 30th '81 R. Shire

Left this morning at the usual time. It is Sabbath Day. The morning is dull and heavy wreathes of mist hang over us. About 10 am we halt at a village for breakfast. Here the men of the village were engaged some in loitering about while two were engaged at a weaving loom making calico. It seemed very arduous

and tedious Employment but time to the African is of
small moment. After three hours stay during which
time a great deal of palaventing [sic] went on
amongst the boatmen about food and after all were
but poorly successful on this score. We again
proceeded on our way but our progress was much
hindered with the constant appeals of paddlers for
food to those who appeared on the banks. We only
made a few miles when we stopped early in the
afternoon at one of Chipibulu's village for the night.
The Chip. son had arrived today on a visit and
enjoyed himself hunting a pig with bows and arrows.
Sometime before we arrived a man was killed by a
buffaloe [sic] which caused some excitement in the
village. The body was buried a few yards from where
we camped. One of the natives came to the bank with
his rattles and presented a savage appearance with a
hat covered over with feathers and locks of hair
hanging from the hat kept up a hideous noise with
shouting and rattling combined, and otherwise going
through a series of dances which was anything but

69

graceful. Ultimately he had to be ordered away from the bank for the monotony of his tones sounded harshly on our ears. All the drums of the village were kept beating through the whole night as tokens of mourning for the dead.

> **Author comment:** individual tribes had their own distinctive beliefs, while sharing other spiritual practices with the local tribes, as Sutherland would shortly discover. Tribal members were, for the most part, highly superstitious, believing that witches lurked among members of the tribe were the source of misfortunes. (Certain tribes in Africa continue to subscribe to occult practices today.) The accused often suffered gruesome deaths or were forced to undergo the muavi ordeal, where they had to ingest muavi, a poison prepared from the bark of a tree native to Africa.[59] If the victim vomited

---

59 "The poison ordeal is an outcome of their belief in the supernatural. It is an appeal to a power outside themselves to judge the case, reveal the right, and punish the wrong-doer. It is part of their religious system and appears to them to be right. The witch-

the poison he was deemed innocent. If
he died by poisoning he was guilty. In a
letter home to his father Sutherland
describes being subjected to this ritual
(Appendix II). The spirits of the dead, it
was believed, could assume the form of
lions or some other ferocious animal.
The natives generally believed in a
higher God, who was worshiped through
various cults. When tribal Chieftains
died, upwards of 100 slaves might be
slaughtered to accompany the deceased
to the next world. The Chieftains' wives
might also join them in death. When
missionary doctors like Dr. Robert Laws
healed native illnesses with western
medicines they were viewed as
magicians. — J. McCracken, pp. 42-43.
"This idea that the missionary had

---

doctor is to them the visible and accessible agent of the ancestral
spirits whom they believe in and worship, and from whom they
think he derives his powers ... The characteristics of the witch-
doctor are a pretended superior knowledge to discern the affairs of
individuals and communities, and an ability to hold intercourse
with the ancestral spirits." *Among the Wild Ngoni*, W. Elmslie, pp.
60-66.

medicine for war, medicine for rain, medicine for good marksmanship, and in short for everything under the sun, was a very prevalent and deep-rooted one."[60]

Additional author comment: The missionaries made lasting impressions among the tribal members when rain was desperately needed and their prayer ("magic") brought rain. But the missionaries steadfastly refused to pray against a rival tribe when asked, instead expounding upon Christ's love of all people, stressing the importance of maintaining peace between tribes.

January 31st 81 R. Shire

Rose this morning with the first streaks of daylight after a very good night's sleep. The drums were still

---

[60] *Daybreak In Livingstonia*, p. 109.

beating and the faint rattling of the charming rattles sounded in the distance, and gradually came nearer until he [the witch doctor] approached us at the fire where we were making coffee. A sign from the cook to go away was speedily complied with and he retrased [sic] his steps. Away we started at about 6 am. The morning was again cloudy a heavy shower of rain fell which lasted only for a few minutes. The sun then broke forth and dispelled the clouds and shone in all his strength. Having finished D. Livingstone's book I took up—*Wanderings in Eastern Africa*. We saw a good many hippos swimming and diving about the River all at a safe distance from the boats. At 11 am we halted for breakfast on the right bank of the River. On the left bank we observed some bucks moving about at the rivers edge. We stayed there two hours and afterwards continued on our way. The afternoon turned out very nice and we enjoyed the scenery around very much but one time we got a sight of a few elephants on the left bank of the river, and further on the Hippos abounded in great numbers in the

River. Stopped on the left bank for the night about 6 pm.

February 1st 81 R. Shire

I managed to get astir this morning before sunrise after enjoying unbroken slumbers. Having taken some precautions on the night previous we were not attacked by the Nyaras ants which exist in countless numbers on the bank, consequently we had no unpleasant dreams, caused by these marauding creatures. Shortly after sunrise we started off at a slow speed the current against us being rather too much for the paddles. The river followed a very serpentine course, meandering to all points of the compass. The banks are studded with giant grasses interwoven climbing plants. A few miles to the right of us are a range of mountains cloaked to its summits with dence [sic] purple of vegetation. Since yesterday morning we have been sailing through a part of the country called the Elephant Marsh during which time

Elephant Marsh

we saw these animals which its name signifies. The day was very fine, a nice cool breeze floated gently with us which kept us very comfortable. At 10:40 am we stopped on the right bank of the River for breakfast. Under the shade of the trees the cooking is carried on under the superintendence of Mr. McIllvaine who also conducts the baking department, making very good scones out of a compound of some sugar, eggs, & flour. Shortly after 1 pm we started on our way through many tortuous windings in the river. At times the current got so strong, that the boats scarcely moved an inch ahead and often receded a few yards until the long grass was got hold of. The boats must keep close by the bank for this purpose. One of our paddlers fell sick this afternoon and his place was left vacant. I filled his place for half an hour but soon exhausted myself at this unusual exercise. We halt on the left bank of the river in an unsheltered spot. A heavy thunderstorm is brewing which will doubtless soon burst upon us.

February 2nd 81 R. Shire

The thunderstorm anticipated the night previous broke out in terrible fury. The rain came down in turrents [sic] and threatened to flood our grassy cabins. By the careful use of mats we avoided being entirely saturated. At both ends of the covering the rain gained access so that we were compelled to roll up our beds and compose ourselves in the center the only place which felt dry. The shades of night had now fallen upon us and everything looked black and dismal, save when the lightnings [sic] vivid glare cast a momentary flash around us. The loud rolls of the thunder as it reverberated among the hills and the incessant torrents of rain was anything but pleasant in the unfavourable [sic] circumstances in which we were placed. And, moreover, this was not the only misfortune, for owing to this humid state of the surroundings the art of cooking had to be dispensed with and we had to content ourselves for the night with a few scraps of dry food. For the same reason the boatmen had to go supperless to bed, if I may call it;

77

they had only mats to lie upon which was ill-suited to be proof against the falling torrents. Early in the evening we devised a plan to have a sleep. Instead of placing our beds in the usual we put them crosswise [sic]. This denied us the privilege of getting our legs stretched as the width of our grass house is not equal to its length. We, however, made the best of a bad job and contented ourselves with our lot. Hanging up one mosquito curtain we both got under it and felt pretty comfortable. This morning I am glad to say we slept tolerably, no rain having dampened our slumbers. Just as daylight dawned I got on foot, the storm had subsided, but the atmosphere was still chargedwith watery vapour. [sic] Coffee was made ready and we enjoyed it immensely after fasting through the past night. The boatmen now began to cook their food and poor fellows they were hungry enough, having to dispense with food the night previous. This unusual proceeding kept us two hours longer than usual so that the sun was far up in the heavens before we started. Ultimately we got started on our way against the stream. On our right we passed a plantation of palm trees and in front of the lofty summits of Mt. Cholo towered high up in the air. The aspect of the right banks in this part presents almost the same unvarying similarity, here a garden of Chimanga, there a covering of thicke [sic] tall grass, now a patch of meadow land; and now a clump of wood composed of short indigenous trees interwoven with various kinds of creeping plants. I spent the greater part of the forenoon in reading News' *Life in Eastern Africa*, a very valuable and no doubt authentic book. About midday a halt was called for breakfast, on the right bank of the river, often our men have scarcely anything to eat, their supplies being exhausted. Our own stores are pretty well run upon also, and if we are much longer on our journey we shall have to suffer for it. After two hours stay we are again away. The sun was now broken in full strength and all our damp clothes are quickly dried. Nothing of note has been noted this afternoon. The boats are speeding along at a good rate. About 6 PM, we stop at a village on the left bank of the river for the night.

February 3rd 81 R. Shire

Rose this morning after a pretty fair sleep. During the night the Hack ants compelled me to alter my position by placing my head where the feet should be. This precaution, however, was successful in thwarting the enemy and after a little composure I fell asleep again. Left this morning at 6 am. The sun soon rose with his burning heat and all nature basked under his genial rays. At 11 am we halted at the village of_____where Chipitula a very warlike chief resides. On landing we shook hands with him, a middle sized man of fierce features. He was attired in a blue shirt, a pair of trousers, and a pair of knee sea boots, one of which might hold both his feet. The village consists of a few huts here and there and one large wooden house in the course of construction. The form of the edifice is rectangular. The height of its walls and breadth respectfully 147 by 78 feet. The work no doubt incurs a great amount of labour [sic], but it is of the poorest architecture. Being detained here rather late in the afternoon we have thought it advisable to stay for the night so that an opportunity may be given to the men to obtain food of some sort, seeing that their stores are exhausted. Chipitula has presented us with two goats. A very generous gift considering that our rations are just about done. He also presented our men with a good many stalks of sugar cane which kept them extracting the juices the most of the night. In vain did the poor fellows wait for the proffered food supply. The morning came still the food failed in coming. To avoid further delay we gave over the greater part of a goat to them which they roasted on some sticks.

February 4th 81 R. Shire

This accomplished we started on our journey leaving Chipitula fast asleep and hoping to fare better at the next village. For four hours the men wrought vigorously when we halted for about an hour to cook some food. The men procured some food at a village close by which they kept until we would reach Masehag village some distance farther on. After 3 hours more we arrived at this chief's village. Having to perform an important business here we stayed to continue our way to Mahate after dinner. Here Mr. Fairly presented Chief Maseha with the present from Dr. Kirk consisting of a breech-loading rifle, 290 rounds of ammunition and some coloured [sic] cloths. Mr. Fairley delivered the address which was interpreted by one of our men big Arimoso.

Author comment: Sutherland's very last entry in his journal is the speech Mr. Fairley gave to Maseha, Chief of the Makolos, on this day. It seems more appropriate to present it here then at the end of the journal, since this is the moment Maseha was presented his gifts. In keeping with a tradition established by David Livingstone decades earlier, a fire arm is among the gifts presented to the Chief.

"To the great and Powerful Maseha, I have
been commissioned by your well-known
friend Dr. Kirk who is the Representative of
the Great and Powerful Queen of England to
thank you for that handsome present—
which you so kindly sent him by Dr. Rankin.
And I have great pleasure in having to
present you in return with a valuable breech-
loading rifle and ammunition from your old
friend and master. At the same time on his
behalf I beg to thank you for the kindness
shown to all English travellers [sic] who
have been passing through your country and
I am quite sure you will give every
assistance that lies in your house to all who
may in the future come within or near your
territory. Trusting that friendly feeling
which has always existed between you and
the members of the Livingstonia mission of
the Free Church of Scotland will always
continue and that you will gain the good will
of those in England. Dr. Kirk and the

Gentlemen out here who are endeavouring
[sic] to open up the country and introduce
trade and education for the benefit of your
people. In conclusion I sincerely wish you a
long and prosperous career and God's
blessing on you and all your people."

—George Fairley, Master of *SS Ilala*

In reply Maseha thanked Mr. Fairly and authorized
him to thank Dr. Kirk for his handsome present.
Maseha in return presented our Company a very
large sheep and sundry provisions for our men. A
word about Maseha. He is a very good looking
specimen of an African. At present we found him
sitting in his veranday [sic]with his numerous wives
beside him. He is a very quiet man well advanced in
years, pretty tall in his bearings and withal of a
generous and kind disposition. He received us kindly
and complied with our request at once. He promised
to supply us with men for carrying our baggage to
Blantyre, and otherwise assisting us. His village
contains a good many well-constructed houses kept

in a very clear state, in fact a beau ideal to any that we have seen in our journey up the River.

February 5th 81 R. Shire

At 8 o'clock the evening of the 4th we arrived at Mtebe our journeys end by the Rivers. We remained in our boats for the night. Close by us the loud snorting of the Hippos soundings harshly in our ears, but we became so accustomed to his grunt eflate that we go off to sleep without any concerns about our safety. This morning we set to work in getting the respective cargoes discharged and placed on the banks to be ready in waiting for the men when they came. Soon

The "cataracts" (or rapids) sections of the
Lower Shire and Zambesi rivers posed
significant challenges for travelers,
necessitating the disassembling of the
steam ships, followed by cumbersome
portages around the turbulent waters.

Aboard the Masheela

after the men came numbering about fifty. After a few preliminaries in the way of partitioning out suitable loads for each individual twenty four men were selected for three Masheela and the remaining number were tolled off for the baggage. We were still eight men short for another Masheela so two of us agreed to take one between us and have time about in being carried. Accordingly we started about 11 am. I got into my Masheela and got along speedily. The road lay along through grass, so thick and so high that it was with great difficulty we could get along. My three companions who were travelling [sic] behind (I say travelling because they had to walk 6 miles to get poles for their Masheelas) and by the time they issued from the forest of grass they were pretty well exhausted. At this juncture I had to get off and walk for now we had come to the base of a hill and we had the ascent to make. Therefore we could not think that the men could possibly carry us up the hill, up, up, up we went over stones and trees at one time turning this way at other that way. At one moment we reached the top of a ridge the next moment we had to go down a little distance and so on. The perspiration by this time expending from every pore in rich effusion. The heat became stifling. The perspiration organs seemed to distend but almost failed to contract. Over our heads the sun goes forth an intense heat so that before the topmast summit was reached I had from sheer thirst to sit-down under

the shade of a tree. A short draught [sic] from a tea
kettle which opportunity was at hand so far restored
me and quenched my thirst – but it was not until I
had rested for 20 minutes and became cooled down
that I could continue the ascent. Still onward and
upward I pressed on and in a very short time reached
the top. I glanced eagerly down the side of the
mountain through the thickly growing trees to see if I
could decipher my companions but no, I at once got
into the Masheela and made off as quickly as possible
down the other side of the hill so that I might get in
haste to some cool, refreshing spring to quench my
parched thirst and at once send relief to my
companions whom I thought would be extremity for
draught [sic] of water. I at once despatched [sic] a
supply, when shortly afterward Mr. McIllvaine came
panting towards me and telling me that Mr. Fairley &
Henderson had given in and that the Masheela be
sent for them at once. We contrived of a little trouble
to get a Masheela sent away. Soon after Mr. Fairley
was carried towards us, he having given in before he

reached the summit of the hill and therefore had to be carried up the steep side of the mountain. Mr. Fairley had his own tale to tell, exhaustion & thirst, etc. The next to come was Mr. Henderson who alike had a similar tale of exhaustion to relate. However a cool fresh drink of the crystal water, followed by a good cup of tea reanimated them again and we got started again up the hill. I now surrendered my Masheela to Mr. Henderson and undertook to walk a few miles. I started off a good sharp pace and the Masheela came after me. The road lay along the side of the hill, shaded from the sun by umbrageous trees and commanding such scenery as is very seldom met with. Giant mountains representing variety of shape and form clothed with the richest vendura. [sic] Steep ravines, wide plains, and beautiful valleys stretched out before us in exquisite taste. For more than an hour I walked.

Author comment: since Sutherland (at this point) is no longer aboard the steamship that he started his journey on, he does not describe the physical obstacles encountered by the famous Dr. Robert Laws (the minister who established Livingstonia I at Cape Maclear) in Laws' first trip up the Shire River in 1875. The *Illala* may have turned around and gone back down the river on this trip. Sutherland is unclear about that. But on trips where the ship's destination was Lake Nyasa, upon reaching the Murchison cataracts, which separated the upper and lower Shire River, the *PS Ilala* had to be disassembled and carried around the rapids. Steamship travelers encountering the Cabora Bassa rapids on the Zambesi River also faced this trial. The length of the portage of the *Ilala* around the Murchison Cataracts was 100 km (65 - 70 miles). Laws hired 600 porters to carry the ship parts, boiler included, up rocky precipices and narrow jungle paths for 10 days, relating how they "toiled desperately over 70 miles of execrable country; not one had deserted as they might have easily done (and) being every article had been delivered safe and unbroken."[61]

---

[61] National Library of Scotland, Item #7907, Dr. Robert Laws Diary Entries 08/31/1875, 09/05/1875, 09/06/1875, and 09/19/1875.

February 6th 81 Blantyre

Slept tolerably the past night on the floor. No mosquitoes disturbed our peaceful slumbers. In the morning we started on our journey to Blantyre and reached it about 3:30 in the afternoon. On arriving we were introduced to several of the members of the Blantyre Mission and also to the representatives of the Livingstonia Company. In a very short time after we arrived three members of the Livingstonia Mission came to Blantyre for the purpose of recovering their health.

February 7th 81 Blantyre

This is a charming spot, a perfect paradise. The ground is laid off in a nice and uniform manner. In the morning I took a round amongst the gardens with Mr. Duncan, the gardener. All kinds of fruit and vegetables for domestic purposes were shown to me in mostly all stages of development. Wheat, potatoes,

Barley, onions, carrots, coffee plants, etc. Flowers of all kinds and colours lined the walks, the whole scene reminds one of home for certainly I have seen nothing so beautiful since I came to Africa. I have been getting a good deal of valuable information from Mr. Duncan, which I hope will aid me in a thousande [sic] ways in my own work at Livingstonia.

February 8th 81 Blantyre

Rose at 6 am and had breakfast at seven in Mr. Duncan's. Afterwards, [sic] visited the gardens, ETC. In the afternoon I visited the school with Mr. McDonald and heard some classes repeat their lessons in their own language.

> **Author comment:** Reverend Duff McDonald was the minister in charge at Blantyre mission. He and his wife (first white woman to arrive in Shire Highlands) were the parents of the first white child born in British Central Africa. Sutherland's mentioning the well-kept grounds at Blantyre is echoed in other biographies, attributing them to the care of Mrs. McDonald.

93

As noted earlier, in spite of having different sponsors, Blantyre (Church of Scotland) and Livingstonia (Free Church of Scotland) frequently coordinated their activities. Sutherland mentions Blantyre Mission taking in Livingstonia staff who had fallen sick at their mission. A modern historian compares these two missions: "The Free Church Mission emphasized educational work and evangelism, while the United Presbyterian Church [Blantyre] came to promote evangelism and church building."[62]

February 9th 81 Blantyre

Spent the greater part of today in writing letters.

February 10th 81 Blantyre

Got up this morning when the bugle sounded for work. Every morning the work people assemble in

---

[62] *Origins and Early Development of Scottish Presbyterian Missions in South Africa (1842 –1865),* Graham A. Duncan, fourth para, p.5.

the school room to hear the roll called. Before the roll is called Mr. McDonald offers up an English and nature prayer. We have breakfast & every morning about 7 o'clock, a very opportune time. I felt very heavy all this day, could scarcely bear my own weight. The day was very hot—which no doubt accounted for it. In the afternoon after a few of us had some rounds of firing the target being a tree with a piece of paper on it. Out of three shots I managed to strike the tree once. The distance was scarcely 100 yards. After this I lay down on my bed for an hour and rose quite refreshed. I have spent a good part of the night in Mr. Duncan's.

February 11th 81 Blantyre

Got up this morning about 6 am. Spent the most of the day in walking about the Garden and field. Mr. Duncan showed me the 1st, 2nd, and 3rd sawings of the Zambesi wheat, English wheat and oats, all of which are coming on with. In the afternoon I went along with him where he was planting Gum trees, and observed the performance closely quite enjoying the way until my attention was arrested by a village. I was here cautioned to stay until my companions came up one by one by one they came in quick succession and here they all came to a dead stand. It was at once opined that we should put up at the village for the night as we could not reach another one before night. We were received by the chief who gave us a house to put up in for the night, etc. We are only too glad to realize that we have at last mounted higher than the buzzing and biting mosquitoes, therefore we hope to have a quiet night. The landscape from this point of the mountain is enchanting. It almost mocks description.

February 12th 81 Blantyre

By a prodigious effort I was able to get out of bed this morning. I just got up in time for breakfast at 7 a.m. In the forenoon I sowed some peas in a brake [furrow]. Spent a while in the afternoon in reading, and a short-time before tea I had a game at cricket with the schoolboys. In the evening some of us had a game at Quartethe and a few of Saukeys. Retired to rest about 10 pm. [**Author comment**: attempts at learning more about these particular games were not successful.]

Sabbath February 13th 81 Blantyre

Spent a very quiet Sabbath. All noise and bustle is hushed on this sacred day. In the forenoon I attended Divine Service conducted in the Native Language. There were perhaps over a hundred present. In the afternoon at 2 p.m. I again attended Divine Service conducted in English. There were 11 Europeans present – 5 of whom belonged to the Livingstonia Company and Mission and 6 to the Blantyre Mission. Mr. McDonald addressed the meeting from Isiah 53.6 "All we like sheep have gone astray."

Monday February 14th 81 Blantyre

Enjoyed most of the day in Gardening. In the morning I had a few turns at the scythe and afterwards planted some balsam cutting along the walks. In the afternoon I saw some orange and granadilla cuttings [a passion fruit] planted by Mr. Duncan and also Lettuces transplanted from beds. The day has been dull and foggy although a splendid day for vegetation.

Tuesday February 15th 81 Blantyre

Left Blantyre this morning at a quarter before 8 am. Our train consisted of two Masheelas and other necessary articles. We rode and walked alternatively. At 2 p.m. we stayed an hour for dinner. We again proceeded on our journey and reached Matope at 7:40 pm. Nothing of any note transpired on the way save that Captain Fairley's Masheela pole broke about a mile from Blantyre. A messenger was at once despatched for another which was soon brought— and we continued on our way. We saw no living specimens of beasts although we observed footprints on the road. About 9 o'clock we had some coffee and eggs and afterwards laid ourselves down to sleep.

Monday February 16th 81 Blantyre

From want of my bed and mosquitoe curtain I suffered some annoyance from the mosquitoes. About 8 a.m. my bed and Dr. Laws box arrived at Matope. A

few minutes afterwards [sic] we started on our
further journey in the large and_____[?] steel boat.
The boat is propelled by 8 oars. Capt Fairley at the
helm. The morning is bright and warm and the
landscape is Enchanting. Large amount of hippos
snorting and snuffing about us, enormous brutes
some of them. At 1 PM we stay on the left-bank of the
river for dinner, a small breeze blew and on starting
the sail and jib was hoisted but we did not get from
the squall for it fell as fast as it rose. The rain also fell
and we were obliged to take down the sail and get the
awning up, etc. At sunset we cast two anchors in the
centre [sic] of the river.

Tuesday February 17th 81 Upper Shire

At the first blink of daylight preparations are made
for a start—and shortly afterwards we were
underway. The morning was wet and the wind
ahead. Progress was very slow indeed. Oftentimes we

went backwards instead of forward. We scarcely managed to go a mile an hour—the current and wind against us. Tonight we stay at the village of Pembi, only 15 miles from Matope thus taking two days to accomplish this distance. Here we introduced ourselves to Mr. Fairley hunter for the LCC who invited us to his house and treated us very hospitably tonight. I have a lingering sore head which compelled me to go to bed very early.

Wednesday February 18th 81 Upper Shire

Slept pretty well during the night not withstanding the headache. This morning I feel much better and almost restored to usual health. The morning is fair but the wind is still ahead of us. How long is this to continue I don't know but the sooner it comes, the better. I must now pass over a few days during which time I was down with fever. On Wednesday Feb 23rd we reached Livingstonia. We were received by the missionary staff and crowds of natives who came and welcomed us. We got a very warm reception from Dr. Laws and the others.

> **Author comment:** considered an enlightened man for his times by modern historians, Laws painstakingly built a reputation for teaching natives trade skills to engage in practical work and earn their way independent from the mission payroll (typically pay was in the form of calico, one yard per day). Laws was unquestionably an evangelist first, but he implemented Livingstone's vision of "the 3-Cs" for native Africans at his missions. Laws spent over 50 years at the three Livingstonia missions. In his 1878 report to the Free Church of Scotland Foreign Missions Committee, Laws identified six areas of work being performed at his mission: (1) Evangelism; (2) Education; (3) Medical assistance rendered to mission staff and, as time passed, more and more for the natives; (4) Carpentry; (5) Agriculture; (6) Journies, which focused on visiting natives in

their villages, what we would consider outreach today.[63]

Thursday the 24th

I slept most of the day. On Friday 25th Dr. Laws showed me over the gardens which are grown over with weeds. The soil is very inferior.[64]

---

[63] National Library of Scotland 7876/244 Robert Laws, report for 1881.

[64] **Author comment:** poor soil conditions aside, the region around Lake Nyasa teemed with many types of raw materials and agricultural products. Cotton, indigo, rubber, gums, drugs, hardwoods like ebony, African teak, mahogany, hard yellow woods, fibres, wheat, rice, Indian corn, millet, sugar, tobacco, vanilla, oranges, mangoes, limes, pineapples, coffee, and tea were local products. See *The Zambesi Basin and Nyassaland*, D. Rankin, p. 256.

Saturday 26th

Prepared some orange cuttings and planted them in a box. Sent Bill to clear out weeds with his hoe. Very quiet here today.

Sabbath Feb 27th

Spent a very quiet day. Services were held for the natives at a quarter past 10, which lasted for three quarters of an hour. In the evening I attended worship in Dr. Laws' Manse. Mr. Johnston at present a guest of Dr. Laws addresses us from the word. "By grace are ye saved." etc

> **Author comment:** a missionary at Livingstonia later shared his observations of the typical worship service —"We had been asked by our carping critics at this time, 'What are the results of your work?' We could not have pointed to a single convert, although the Mission had been already three years in the district. To all

appearance it was a failure. From the chief and the councillors we had stolid indifference, and direct veto against educating the children, or moving about to preach the Gospel, and from many of our next neighbours. We were receiving marks of base ingratitude and opposition. Of stated work, there was not much. We were denied access to every village save two outside the area of Hoho, as the district in which we lived was called. On the station we were meeting daily with men and women, and youths and maidens who were employed in House building. To these we had the opportunity of speaking about spiritual things. There were the boys in the house as servants who collected for worship and oral instruction every day. A few young men outside began to take an interest in these services and attended. From them grew a stated service on Sabbath, to which by and by others came, and although open preaching of the Word had been proscribed, we gradually came out more boldly and our service was tolerated, and in turn became an object of interest to others abroad. Only a few of the women came, and the men were fully armed. The service was often very uproarious. The dogs snarled and fought with each other, and when this took place the backers of the different dogs whistled and encouraged them. Often audible remarks followed the reading of passages or parts of the address. Sometimes a man would get up and declare that it was all lies and demand cloth as they had heard enough of the Gospel. Some came out of curiosity; others came having the impression that we gave cloth to all who attended; and sometimes spies were sent by the chief's councillors to see and report what was done. This was known to us for some time, but we did not think any evil would come of it, until the rumour got abroad that we were inciting the slaves to revolt against their masters ... The rumour arose from the Tumbuka slaves having begun to attend the meetings, and afterwards discussing the teaching of the Ten Commandments."[65]

Monday February 28th 81

Spent most of the day in going about doing little. Caught a snake three-feet long. Kept the boys busily

---

[65] *Among the Wild Ngoni*, Elmslie, p.148.

weeding the whole day. I feel very dull since I came
here.

Tuesday March 1st

Rose this morning when the bugle sounded for work.
After enjoying a long sleep visited the Garden and got
the boys on to weeding as usual. I am afraid the
orange cuttings are not to thrive with me, along with
Hugh I went in the afternoon and tied up some gum
trees that were leaning too much. Had a walk w Dr.
Laws in the Evening.

Wednesday March 2nd

Wandered about the Station doing small jobs. Had a
walk two miles distant to Garden and got four
women and three garden boys to hoe the grass. I
returned at mid-day pretty well fatigued by walking

under a hot sun. In the evening I attended the weekly prayer meeting in the manse.

Thursday March 3rd

Started this morning for the garden with turnip seed in my hand, but I lost the way so I returned. In the afternoon I started taking along with as guide my own boy. He took the same route as I did in the morning but I did not go far enough on the way. I sowed from Bronze Swedes on the flat in rows 2 feet apart. About 5 P.M. I returned to the Station taking 35 minutes on the way. In the Evening I visited the *Ilala* to see Capt Fairley who is bad with fever. Found him pretty well.

Saturday March 5th 81

The duty of calling the roll in the morning and afternoon now revolves around me since Mr. Kess left. I just got ready when the bugle sounded so I hastened to the stove and got the roll and called it. The work people afterwards went to their duties. The joiners to the shop. The sawyers to sent off to the far garden to finish their hoeing and sowing. About 9 a.m. I went off to the garden taking with some peas for the purpose of sowing. The plot of ground that was cleaned was sown with Swedish and Greystone turnips, also the peas spoken of. The weather is very dry and the turnips may be hindered from germinating but the spot where they are sown is not moist in itself so they have a pretty fair chance. I left the garden about 11-30 intending to reach the garden at 12 noon to pay the work people and left the gardeners to finish the sowing. The afternoon is given as a half-Holiday to the workers, so I set to work in mending my stockings one pair of which nearly baffled me with holes but I persevered and succeeded in sealing up for a time the well-worn worsted. After darkness set in I take to Reading or writing but generally at 8 o'clock sleep lays hold upon me and obedient to the call of nature I get into bed. There to perspire like a bull until sleep makes me insensible to it. Effect, I must shift my shirt every night as it is generally damp with perspiration.

Sabbath March 6th 81

Another return of the blessed Sabbath. I attended the native service at 10:15 in the school room. Dr. Laws spoke to the people. The attendance was rather smaller than the previous Sabbath. In the afternoon I went along to the Mepangai 5 miles distant in the "Meina." In the boat there were eight individuals. We arrived at the village after 30 mins. sailing. The bell was rung for the meeting but few turned out. The boys went along to the houses but few seemed to care about coming. I opened the meeting by giving out a hymn. Afterwards, Albert, one of the school teachers, engaged in prayer and addressed the meager company. Taking from his text a passage from Mark's

Gospel. All through the service one native sat before us working away at a mat quite unconcerned about our presence. Others again sat and listened to the word attentively. The men were most attentive, the women being more or less annoyed with their children. After the address I gave out the hymn (*When Mothers of Salem*) which we sang heartily, none of the village people joining in. After the hymn was sung Albert closed the meeting with prayer and we departed reaching Livingstonia about 6 o'clock being absent 2 hours and a half. In the morning I had tea with Dr. Laws and worship. He spoke for a few minutes from John Gospel 17th chapter, Christ intercessory prayer.

March 7th 81

Spent a rambling sort of night tossing about from side to side and could not sleep. Glad when daylight came in that I might get on foot. Just as I had given myself a wash the bugle sounded so hastened to call the roll.

Afterwards I engaged a few men to cut steamer fuel
and I sent the garden boys to the process of weeding.
I myself spent the most of the day in putting handles
in two broken spades. I laboured hard to get the
necessary turns in the wood but failed to get it to my
satisfaction. I find much enjoyment in the work I have
to do and the variations in it makes it all the more
delightful. One day in the garden, another while I am
in the store, occasionally in the cookhouse, how and
again in the School. All and Sunday engages my
attention. Tonight I visited the school and found the
scholars with their teachers busy at their lessons for
the following day. Shortly afterwards Dr. Laws put in
his appearance and went over the reading lesson.
Before leaving he gave them a few rounds of exercise
which was gone through by the teachers and scholars

with great precision. About eight o'clock I find my way into the double decker to prepare for bed.

March 8th 81

I failed to sleep the last night but tossed about upon my bed immense perspiration. Glad when morning came. At the first sound of the bell I hastened to call the roll afterwards betooke myself to the joiners shop to finish my job with the spade handles. In the afternoon I came across a barrow a good deal worse of the wear. However the wheel was the only part of it that seemed to be worst. I at once hurled the barrow to the joiners shop amid the laughing and shouting of the apprentices for the spokes of the wheel were broken and the shod was just hanging on to the wood by one nail. Obtaining a screw key I at once got the wheel separated and began to make new spokes. The job will no doubt cost me some trouble but I am determined to make an attempt. I took a walk down to the beach and there I saw Dr. Laws with some boys casting the net into the Lake. After the net was cast a storm began to brew so the net was at once hauled in and spread on the beach, having enclosed into meshes four fishes, a substantial breakfast for one person, that is to say if they are not at all bones, as a good many that I have eaten predominated in bones. The net being secured we proceeded to the school where the apprentices and scholars were being drilled in their lessons. In the evening rain began to fall, the first we have had for a week. After such an intense heat for the past week the present rain proves very injurious to health as it gives rise to miasma.

Wednesday March 9th 81

The past night I had a refreshing night's sleep. Felt a slight headache in the morning. Dr. Laws recommended me to take some quinine which I did. After calling the roll I proceeded to the joining shop and commenced working at my wheel for the most of the day making an_____[?] visit to the garden to look after the garden boys, and have a peep at the few sensitive plants which I have under my care. In the afternoon the famous wheel was finished, the shod put on with little trouble. I drove four mails in the shod which I found will last a short time. The barrow looks quite well after its renovation. After tea I went down to the lake and helping the boys got the net into the water. The net—which is 300 yards long—takes

MANDALA HOUSE, NEAR BLANTYRE

Typical "Manse" or "Big House," where clergy lived
on mission grounds in Africa.

some time to it is got into the boat so as to be in right
position for casting. When all is ready the boys start
off with the canoe, one end of the net kept on shore.
The canoe goes out a certain distance and then comes
back with the other end to the shore after forming a
semicircle with the net. At both ends we beginning to
haul the net and bring it on shore. Tonight we have
been successful in getting five fishes, only a good
breakfast for two persons if not of the long kind. Dr.
Laws handed them over to me tonight for turn about
is fair play. Afterwards I went to the school and heard
Tommy Falconer repeat his lessons correctly. At
seven o'clock I went along to the Wednesday night
prayers meeting in the manse.

THE *ILALA* ON THE ZAMBEZI

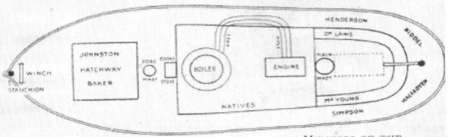

PLAN OF THE *ILALA*, SHOWING WHERE THE MEMBERS OF THE
EXPEDITION SLEPT

Thursday March 10ᵗʰ 81

The most of this day I have been drilling about the station to little purpose, simply looking over the workers and keeping them in Employment. In the morning I tried on my hand at baking. I succeeded fairly well but after my loaf was fixed it tasted of Fatanic [?] acid in excess. This unfortunate occurrence I mean to rectify on the next occasion. I find now is the best time for making experiments as I am alone, but I hope to be an adept-at-baking before the other artisans come from Blantyre.

Friday March 11ᵗʰ 81

My work today was chiefly in looking after the workers but it was very tiresome with so little to do. We had an awful heavy shower today for about 3 hours. The water gauge measures 2 5/8 inches.

Thursday March 17th 81

Ever since Friday last my notes are few. On Sabbath
along with Mr. Harkness and the boat I went to
Mepangay village. Albert conducted the services as
usual, the audience being somewhat better than on
the previous. On the evening Dr. Laws gave us a fine
sermon on the words, "I Am Debtor." Tuesday
morning I was knocked down with fever which
continued to Thursday morning. Got up.

Friday March 18th 81

Uneventful day. Today 5 couples were married. All
the members of the Mission were busily engaged in
making preparations for the marriages, such as
decorating the school, preparing the dinner, etc. In the
afternoon at 3 o'clock the school was crowded. The
brides and the bridegrooms sat in front and the
members of the mission sat in full view of them. Dr.
Laws conducted the ceremony in the native language.

One of the bridegrooms during the course of the ceremony got rather nervous and fainted, coming down to the ground with a heavy knock. He speedily came to and was able to bear up to the end of the affair. Afterwards we entertained to dinner about 60 including as many strangers as we could well treat to a part of the dinner. The mission presented the newly married couples with a large goat, coffee, and other dainties which was ravenously devoured. In the evening the Magic Lantern views were displayed to the great delight of young and old, etc etc

March 22nd 81 Tuesday

Not much doing these days. Work at a standstill. Longing to get away to Bandawe, our future station. Today I commenced making a box for the wreath for Mr. Johny Gunn's grave. I also finished a drainspade [?] which kept me working a long time.

Author comment: Mr. Gunn was the agriculturist at Livingstonia who preceded Sutherland, holding the position Sutherland filled. Gunn died on April 01, 1880, just before his term in Africa was to expire. A colleague who was familiar with his work wrote of Mr. Gunn: "he had not only superintended his own department, but had acted as a very efficient teacher in the school; and having devoted considerable time and attention to the language, he was able to address a meeting fluently and to attend natives visiting the station . . . by firmness and kindness in his dealing with the natives, as well as by his addresses to them in his own language, he had completely won their affection and respect."
Daybreak in Livingstonia, J.W. Jack, p. 135.

Wednesday March 23rd 81

Rose this morning as the bugle sounded. Went direct and called the roll. Then had coffee and returned to the house for a few minutes to devotions. Afterwards went to the joiner shop to continue the box I commenced yesterday. I planted some seeds today in pots, Apricots, Plums, or Prunes, French plums, cherry seeds: peaches, nespole etc. I was kept pretty busy all the day doing small things. In the evening after tea news was brought to us that the goat was dead—and lying some distance from the Station. All hands were up and got lamps and a ladder to carry him in. Before we got 100 yards we met the goat herd coming to the station. We brought him to the Dr. and he was found to have fever, and had been lying on the ground until he was nearly starved. Someone seeing him so thought he was dead and brought the false report. Wednesday evening is held as a prayer meeting in the manse. The subject of prayer was for Albert, who is about to make public profession of his faith, by Baptism.

Saturday March 26th81

On Friday afternoon I was laid down with a slight touch of fever, however this morning I rose quite well. My duties today have been very light merely to see if the boys were attending to their work in the garden. They at present collected the dried weed heaps and burning them. Today I made a lot of lemon cuttings. After 12 Noon there is nothing done. In the evening we made a cast of the net and Enclosed a goodly number of fishes.

Sabbath March 27th 81

I attended the native service and enjoyed it immensely. Although I could not understand the language but from the fact that the first Baptism of a native at Livingstonia took place. Dr. Laws spoke long to the people before he administered the rite of Baptism. Before Albert was baptized he declared to the large audience his faith in Christ with earnestness. After this the Dr. baptized him. The people looked on somewhat in bewilderment having never seen the like before. After the service I made for bed as quickly as possible, a cold chill passing through my body. This was a sure sign of fever. I felt somewhat bad all the afternoon. Towards Evening I rose and sat in a chair for a short time but feeling weak I had to return to bed.

ALBERT NAMALAMBÉ
The first convert in the
Livingstonia Mission

Author comment: in a biographical account of
the Livingstonia Mission entitled *Daybreak in
Livingstonia* the baptism of Albert is described
as follows: "Sabbath March 27th – This is a red
letter day in the history of Livingstonia Mission.
By the blessings of God the work of the past
years has not been for naught, nor has He

126

suffered His word to fail. or long we have been seeing the working of God's work in the hearts of not a few; and now, by God's grace, one has been enabled to seek baptism as a public profession of his faith in Jesus Christ. Last Sabbath Dr. Laws intimated that Albert Namamlambe' would be baptized today. The school was crowded and the attention throughout the whole service was intense … Dr. Laws asked Albert to address the people. This he did in a humble way, and with a respect for the older people which gained the attention of all. He told them the reasons why he sought baptism and his desire to obey God's law. He had been living among them, he said, and they knew if he were speaking the truth. He pleaded earnestly with all to accept of Christ's mercy …Prayer was offered, after which Namamlambe' was baptized in the name of the three—one God by the name of Albert. God bless him and keep him was the earnest prayer of each member of the Mission present on the occasion." It should be noted that this first baptism happened five full years following the establishment of Livingstonia at Cape Maclear.

Monday March 28th 81

I rose this morning quite well, having enjoyed a nice sound sleep and today I have been going about a good deal, but kept out of sun under the shade of houses. Tonight I have a tendency to fever again.

Tuesday March 29th 81

I never slept a wink last night owing to the roving condition of my imagination. Would that the unmerciful malaria would abandon this country. I laboured assiduously to combat my opponent but the full force of the will could not contend with the innumerable thoughts that pass so quickly through my mind: therefore I kept awake all night—finding it entirely useless to close my eyelids. How true the words of Byron, "Thoughts we cannot bridle, but force their way against the will." Today the *Ilala* left for Bandawe with a heavy cargo of the Station flithing

[?]. Dr. Laws & Mrs. Laws went along with her. Mr. R. Reid [**Author note**: Reid is initially listed as "Carpenter" in the Mission roster before being documented as an invalid later in 1881] joins and also his workman left for Bandawe. Mr. Harkness [Engineer of *Ilala*] and I have been left alone at the Station to look after the property. We expect the steamer back in a fortnight when I shall go along and leave Mr. Harkness alone at Livingstonia. Tonight I am partially recovered from fever.

Thursday 31 March 1881

As usual the previous night I was kept from sleeping by inopportune thoughts. The Law of Association of Thoughts however good in its place does not do during sleeping hours so I am extremely in sorrow that it should take place with me. My will is weak so that I can't overcome the indomitable nuisance. However the best cure for it is hard work and that is

129

what I require. Today I got the wreath put on Mr. Gunn's grave Enclosed in a wooden frame with glass front and built round with brick. I left the brick unfinished and intend to resume it next morning. In the evening I made a few pancakes which tasted middling.

> **Author comment:** James Sutherland's self-described 'inopportune thoughts' arise as he decorates the grave of the person he replaced at Livingstonia. Is he bothered by depression? Loneliness? Fear? He does not say.

Friday April 1st 1881

This is the anniversary of my predecessor's death, Mr. Gunn. Today I finished building bricks around the wreathe on the head of his grave. I have been going about as usual seeing how things were doing and making preparations for Bandawe. In the evening Mr. Harkness and I tried on our hands in doctoring a sickle woman who had a pain in her hip. We gave her

Seidlith [sic] powder to taste her mouth and right her stomach.

Saturday 2nd April 81

Things are moving along well as could be expected on the station. I spent a good part of the forenoon in the garden making preparations for Bandawe. The linseed sown a week ago in the Dr.'s garden is now an inch above the ground. In the afternoon we had a marandah [?] on a runaway wife. The said person was one of the wives of Sidej, a member of Makanura. She stole away on the night of the 31st of March what hour is uncertain and remained aloof from her husband until the evening of the first of April. On the morning of the 1st of April the disconcerted husband came to Mr. Harkness for sympathy, taking along with him Bill—the landlord of Sidej to make known the facts of the case. During the whole of Friday the case was dormant but on Saturday at 2 o'clock Sidej appeared in the double decker and implicated Bill as having something to do with the disappearance of the woman. Bill was immediately sent for also the Nkari wife and Chimalolo, Chief. When all appeared upon the scene of the conflict Albert was chosen as the interpreter and Mr. Harkness to do the evidence. Bill on being questioned said that on one occasion he sent away Sidej's wife on the authority of her husband to work in his garden to repay him for the food he was giving to Sidej, but at the time he did not send her away as was supposed when the rumours reached our band that Bill was implicated. Bill on referring us to Nkari Mr. Harkness asked her about running away. Before going away she told Bill not to tell her husband where she was and Bill promised that he would not. Her reason for going away was for fear of her husband whom she thought would kill her. Sidej as we may here remark intended to go home on the day that his wife was amissing, [sic] but he deferred going for a day or two to see if the missing link would return. Chimolo on being questioned responded that Bill came to him on the morning after the Nkari had

132

gone away, asking him if he saw Sidej's wife. He said no. In the afternoon Chimalolo asked Bill if <u>he</u> saw the Nkari yet. No, was the response. Chimalolo said he was astonished at Bill after hearing the evidence. Sidje speaking on his own behalf said he done nothing to his wife that might cause her to go away but that Bill had stolen his wife. The weight of the Evidence was against Bill as being guilty of a falsehood with intent to deceive. A fine was imposed upon Bill by Mr. Harkness (Interim Superintendent of the Station) to the amount of 2 / arrears of wages for two weeks and to cease work until such a time as will be found to be convenient to engage him again. The husband and wife was dismissed leaving the matter in the hands of the Chief Makanjira to settle it.

Monday April 4th 81

Today I have been in a feverish state good for nothing. In the forenoon I went to bed for a few hours

and felt much refreshed when I rose. Sidje and his
wives left here for his own village on Sabbath.

Tuesday April 5ᵗʰ

The *Ilala* arrived from Bandawe at 9 P.M. on the
previous night. The *Ilala* experienced heavy weather
on her return voyage, the wind blowing strongly
right ahead. Today my duties very slight as usual, but
now seeing that the steamer has returned, I will have
to see after the cargo and get it shipped. There was a
strong gale blowing all day, so that lake is the
roughest condition that I have seen it since I came to
Livingstonia. The bay is quite sheltered from all
winds by the hills and islands except the west, but the
westerly winds are not prevalent here. With regard to
health I am pretty well today.

Wednesday April 6th 81

Today I have been engaged in getting the steamer's cargo to the beach. It consisted of timber principally with sundry other things for Bandawe. The weather is very unsettled just now. Strong gales of wind blowing night and day. If such weather should continue I may look out for a sickenet [sic] going to Bandawe in the *Ilala*, but let us hope for the best.

Thursday April 7th 81

This afternoon I got word from Capt. Fairley that the steamer was to start on the morrow. This unlooked for event made me hurry up to get my thing on board. I soon got a few boxes filled with young plants but to my surprise the steamer's hold could not contain the half of them so they were left behind. I therefore had to leave them in charge of Ntanibo for an indefinite period. The weather here again becomes

135

fine. The wind has fallen and the sun, though absconded for two days has again sent down his genial rays. This change in the weather has induced Capt. Fairley to make a start tomorrow.

Friday April 8th 81

The steamer left Livingstonia this morning for Bandawe shortly after 8 A.M. The morning was fair and beautiful. The lake was calm and peaceful and the prospect was enticing. The sun's rays shone brightly on the rocky heights of the numerous islands and heathlands which skirts the shores of the lake. Gaily the *Ilala* sped on her way at full speed now and again giving a dip to her bulwarts in the water. On she went till a quarter past two in the afternoon when the Captain put into a lagoon and anchored for the day—to continue our journey on the morrow. None onboard suffered from sea-sickness, the lake being too calm. We had on board a few passengers from

Bandawe among whom was a man and his two wives. After tea a few shots were fired at hippos, none of which took effect; owing to them being too great a distance from the ship. The evening onboard is spent in reading.

> **Author comment:** while it is not explicitly stated by Sutherland, the transfer of the Livingstonia mission from Cape Maclear to Bandawe is happening at this time. Based on passing references in various documents, it appears the new mission was fully operational in October 1881.

Saturday April 9th 81

Left the lagoon this morning at six A.M. A favourable breeze sprung up which filled all the sails and carried us along at the rate of _____ knots. Sitting on the forepart of the decks I beheld a most gorgeous sight — the rising rays of the sun shining upon the irregular summits of the distant hills. The whole range of hills for a considerable space of time was one vast panorama, which excited feelings of intense admiration in the spectator along his part of the West Coast a vast plain of swamps stretch out for many miles until it terminates at the base of the hills I speak of. Proudly the *Ilala* skimmed over the rising surf rolling betimes from side to side but not in any way exciting the membranes of the stomach to make them dispense with any of its contents. For my part I enjoyed the journey this far immensely, the weather being all that could be desired. At half-past one P.M. the *Ilala* anchored safely in the noted bay of Kota Kota, a hotbed of slavery. Here Captain Fairley and I went ashore and were received on the beach by scores of natives and Arabs. We at once made for the house of the Arab Chief Qumbe. We were here received by his men of state and were shown seats on the floor of the verandah. Qumbe on knowing of our visit reappeared from his mansion and shook our hands. Ioao, one of the steamer hands, acted as our interpreter. A word on the appearance of the Chief.

He wore a long, white robe down to his feet and placing his feet on when he walked he had two pieces of wood with a curve at the toes and a hole in which there was a short piece of wood which went up between the large toes and then a nut was screwed down so as to keep the wooden shoes on the feet. When he walked the wood went clap, clap against his heels, on his head he wore the true Arab style of convening a small crown Hat with a large_____[?] round his forehead. He is a man of rather more than middle age with features not all inhuman like as he really is. We could not detect any characteristic in the physiogony of his face that would border on suspicion. One rather formidable necessity was the massive row of front teeth which projected from the upper jaw, but taken as a whole he was a good specimen of an Arab. On both sides of the Entrance to the house under the verandah sat his prime ministers and officers of state. On his left sat the tailor sewing at some white calico, on his right another with a long string of beads counting them. At a little distance from the Chief two Arabs were engaged at a game at drafts while scores of natives on both sides sat with their mouths and ears open listening to what we were saying through the interpreter. We rose to leave but the Chief who was going to another village invited us to come with him. All his officers and men of state clothed in white robes followed the Lordship to the neighbouring palace. On arriving at a similar house to that of the other we were asked to have a seat. While we were seated a little boy brought a large pot and a jug to the Chief. We at once surmised was sour goats whey and curd. I took a long draught of it being very thirsty owing to the intense heat but Mr. Fairley not relishing the sourness of the contents took but little of it and the little that he did take seemed to stick to his moustache which created a general outburst of feeling amongst the assembled crowns. After partaking of this unlooked-for hospitality we made a respectful bow and parted from him. This Chief possesses 15 large dhows [sailing vessels outfitted with one or two masts, similar to Chinese junks] for carrying slaves to the East of the Lake from whence they are driven to the coast. He carries on a large trade in human flesh and is greatly enriched by it. Two large dhows came into the bay in the afternoon from the opposite side of the Lake for fresh cargoes of humanity. Only one slave was seen today with a piece of wood on his neck though no doubt many in the numerous villages were not seen by us. This Chief is the most powerful on the Lake and never since I came into Africa did I see so many native houses with such a large population. On leaving the Chief we had a walk for two miles on a visit to hot springs. We saw several of them some were just hot enough for the fingers while the temperature of one we visited was hot enough to boil an egg. On satisfying ourselves with our visit to them we retraced our steps where we spend the rest of the afternoon. We will stay in Kota Kota Bay until Monday morning.

Author comment: Sutherland's account of his encounter with slave trade operations in Lake Nyasa confirms that the highly publicized demise of the slave trade was premature. Not long before Sutherland's arrival in Africa, Sultan Barghash bin Said in Zanzibar had issued a series of increasingly stringent "edicts"

142

purportedly prohibiting slave trading, more specifically, the elimination of the slave markets in Zanzibar and other major centers where slaves were sold. But he did this reluctantly, under great pressure from British officials. Not only had the Sultan regularly taken bribes to turn a blind eye to slave trading, the Sultan's enforcement authority did not extend much beyond the coastline of East Africa, holding little sway in places like the Lake Nyasa region. The scourge of slave trading was not a thing of the past while Sutherland was in Africa. Arab slave traders who had initially been impressed by the new arrival of the *Lady Nyasa* (she was viewed as some sort of powerful gunship), soon realized the ship carried little *real* enforcement authority. There would be no direct interdiction of the dhows crammed with slaves crossing the Lake towards the eastern shore for transfer to Zanzibar. The traders went back to acting with impunity, at times even mocking the steam ship's presence while slave trading continued like before, out in the open.[66] At the founding of

---

[66] **Author comment:** the response of the Arab slave traders and the natives to the presence of the *Ilala* on Lake Nyasa in the early days of the Livingstonia Mission is discussed in detail in *Daybreak in Livingstonia*, pp.53–61. The author refers to, "great consternation

Livingstonia in 1875 the Free Church of
Scotland's Foreign Missions Committee
addressed slavery in Article IX of its
Instructions to Lake Nyasa Mission Party under
the heading Active Interference With the Slave
Trade:

On this difficult question no rule can be laid
down, except this, which is absolute and to
be observed by all members of the party,that
active interference by force initiated on your
side is in no case to be resorted to. By
showing the people in kindly, loving
concilliatory ways, that they are acting
against their own interests, and destroying
themselves in carrying on this trade, more
will be gained in the long run, than by any
armed interference with Arab caravans. It
should never be forgotten that the first shot
which is fired in any hostilities against Arab
or native slave-dealers will do more to

---

among the natives," when the steam ship was perceived as a "fire
ship" by the locals watching it move rapidly through the water
without the assistance of sails or paddles.

paralyse the varied efforts of the member of the expedition than any temporary success in the liberation of slaves can possibly counterbalance. Fire arms were to be used only in self defence.[67]

Sabbath April 10th 81

During the whole of this stay we lay snugly at anchor at Kota-Kota Bay. I did not go ashore at all during the day. In the afternoon our attention was attracted towards the shore by loud sounds of voices. We noticed a great many people on the shore and were led to believe that gangs of slaves had arrived from the neighboring villages around ready for

---

[67] *East Central Africa, Livingstonia* (Free Church, Edinburgh) 1876, p. 28.

shipment on the following morning in the dhows that had come in the previous night.

Monday April 11th 81

Left Kota-Kota this morning at 6:20. The wind favoured us from the south so that all sails were set and the *Ilala* sped on her way at a good rate. At breakfast time I felt squeamish and soon vomited the contents of my stomach. Not being able to partake of any food I at once got my bed spread and lay down. At intervals I vomited again. During the forenoon the sea washed the decks of the *Ilala* and more than once I had to shift my position in order to escape a drubbing but with all my care the pea overcame me and gave my bed a drubbing. About two hours before we reached our desired haven we observed on the shore the flash lights of the mirror which indicated that all was well. The Capt. of the *Ilala* returned the compliment by flashing his looking glass in the sun. At half-past three we put safely into Bandawe bay and very soon got ashore. Speedily my baggage followed and now I am safely housed in a temporary house here. As far as I have seen of the place its position etc., it is much superior to Livingstonia being placed as it is on the top of a gently rising hill. I had tea with the Dr. and Mrs. Laws.

Tuesday April 12th 81

I got up this morning and commenced duties at 6 a.m. I first called the roll and afterwards went along to Dr. Laws who was planning out a road for a distance of 3 miles. The road begins with a breadth of 20 feet and gradually narrows to 12 feet when it becomes stationary at this distance to the end. After 20 women are engaged to clear the bush, a stiff job with the roots of trees. I have been living of the breadth [?] and overseeing the work so that the road is kept high in

147

the centre and sloping down in the form of a crescent. The object of this mode of road making is to defend it a very little from the torrents of rain that visits this island. Plenty of work laid out for me to do the____[?] of it would take me all my time to perform it. The hour of halting was very welcome to me, being very weary with going about. A word about Bandawe. This new Station is situated on a narrow neck of land partially surrounded by water at a height of 200 feet above the Lake. On the whole though in its wild state there is some charm about it. First of all it is exposed to the bracing breezes from the North and South, which renders it comfortable. A full view of the Lake can be had North and South, etc. Time alone can make it a pleasant spot and clear away the dense and almost impenetrable brush.

Wednesday, Thursday, and Friday April 13th, 14th, 15th 81

I have been of very little use in the way of working, having suffered from fever. During the forenoon I generally took a walk along to see how the road is progressing but in the afternoons I must keep indoors out of the hot sun. Today Friday I feel pretty well, having partaken of food more freely than on other days. Ever since I came to Bandawe the wind has been blowing strongly from the South. On Tuesday the *Ilala* had to make for Mitakay for shelter, a distance of 30 miles from Bandawe. She has not since returned.

Saturday April 16th 81

After sleeping soundly all the night I rose this morning feeling all well again. I called the roll and afterwards went to superintend the road markers. The road is progressing very well and about 200 yards of it is finished. The Dr. showed me a field of say 6 acres which he wanted to get cleaned, he also pointed out the side of the cattle kraal and_____[?] who is intended to be constructed someday. At noon we paid the men and women for their fortnight's work 2 fathoms [of calico cloth]. The rest of the day is given as a half holiday.

Monday April 18th 81

Yesterday was spent very quickly as it should be. I enjoyed reading and meditation very much. In the forenoon Dr. Laws addressed several hundreds of all sizes in front of his house. They all listened attentively to the words that were spoken. In the evening Dr. Laws addressed us in English from Isiah III. He dwelt on the life of our Master on earth. In our work on the mission he reminded us of prayer and pains with patience as being the best things for bringing down God's blessing on our work and the people around. Today I have been engaged in making the road. In the morning I took on over 200 hands for the various departments of work. I myself kept oversight of 74 women in levelling the road and 8 men at the cutting of stumps for the road is progressing rapidly.

> "At times it must have seemed to almost every missionary that the one thing there was no time or place for was formal missionary work. Traveling, obtaining supplies, arranging the dispatch of mail, building, gardening, digging irrigation canals, ensuring your water supply or your daily meal were all such engrossing and tiring occupations, let alone having babies, coping with illnesses, and learning a language. Yet all this was subsidiary to the great work they had come to do: preaching, the making of converts, the establishment of a Christian Church."[68]

---

[68] Victorian Missionary, Oxford On-Line, *The Victorian Missionary,* by Adrian Hastings, p.16.

Tuesday April 19th 81

After coffee I went away to superintend the road-making and made pretty fair progress. The stumps of trees were a continual hindrance in the way. The day was very warm. Still there was a little wind that kept a cool draught of air about me. The rainy season appears to be over now.

Wednesday April 20th 81

Went this morning and continued all the day at the making. In the forenoon Mr. Paterson arrived from Mitaka on a flying visit and in the afternoon the *Ilala* came also from Mitaka Bay. In the evening I went on board the *Ilala* for a while.

Thursday April 21ˢᵗ 81

The steamer left this morning at 5 a.m. And I am alone now to conduct the work of the new Station. As usual I had to look after the road-making which on the whole is making good progress. In addition to this work I have the Malonda [?] and books to attend to, etc. Tonight I have been trying to understand the books and get the accounts written down. In the afternoon Mr. Reid and I shifted to the house which the Dr. and Mrs. Laws tenanted while here. It is large and commodious but pestered with ants, etc The wind is blowing strongly from the South tonight and it is to be hoped the *Ilala* is safe in Kota Kota Bay.

Friday April 22ⁿᵈ 81

I enjoy a sound sleep every night now, having plenty of manual exercise. Today I have been at the road

153

again. The stumps of trees are a great drawback to progress. However two or three days more will finish the allotted distance. The surface bush I hope will be cleared away tomorrow. This day has been very pleasant—a strong breeze and a dull sky made the atmosphere very cool, indeed. I am afraid the *Ilala* is still in Kota Kota Bay from stress of weather.

Saturday April 23rd 81

Today has been very boisterous and stormy. Heavy showers of rain fell during the forenoon which somewhat retarded the work. The surface bush of the road was all cleared away this morning but as the stumps of trees were not all cleared away the making of the road could not be carried on so I brought the women to the station and set them to clear the bush so as to form afield. The latter half of the day is given as a holiday. I spent the afternoon in Reading & writing, and in the twilight Mr. Reid and I went down to the beach where the intended breakwater is to be built. The waves that swept the beach reminded me of my own native shores during a swell in the bay.

Sabbath 24 April 81

In the forenoon Mr. Reid conducted the native service. Over 150 people assembled to hear the word of God. At the close of the service I sought to interest the boys that gather in great numbers and pictures of Bible stories. Though I could not instruct them in their own language I benefited by the names of the several pictures. Boys I am told are the best to learn the language from as they give a distinct sound to the names. In the afternoon Mr. Reid and I went to Marengaj village three miles distant. On arriving at the village we found that the village was burnt to the ground. The cause of the disaster is probably that some michevious [sic] person or persons set a light to one of the houses and owing to the strong gale that was blowing at the time it would speedily reach the

155

other houses. Strange to say the village was burnt during the day and and [sic] no clue could be got as to the perpetrators of the deed. The men of the village were busy erecting new houses at the command of the Chief. They left their work and came to the meeting. About 100 people, assemble under a tree, and Mr. Reid conducted their service. On our return walk we took a circuitous round along the sandy beach of the Lake. The white culling breakers rushed imperviously against the beach, the Lake being in a storm. How very like the Ackergill Sands [*today the Sands are a scenic reserve in Scotland*] are the shores of the Lake as it stretches for miles and miles along the Lake, a vast mass of pure sand. Ultimately we reached out our house quite tired after the walk. In the evening Mr. Reid held a meeting in the house with his work boys. This closed the day's proceedings.

Monday April 25th 81

Today I have looking [sic] after lots of small about the station, such as planning a small cook house superintending the women cleaning the bush, the clearing of a small plat of ground in a moist place for seed, and the sowing of peas. Mostly every day we have patients come to us for medicine. The worst cases are abscesses in the feet and legs, some of which are so large that it causes us to turn aside from looking at them. Mr. Reid has this important duty to discharge, but he feels inability to do justice to the aching sores of the poor heathen. Salts are a familiar medicine to young children with bad stomachs, etc. There was a case today of a woman who was carried for a good distance because of a large abscess under the ankle of her right foot. Poulticing is the only remedy we can prescribe in such cases. In the forenoon of today I had a slight touch of fever but through walking and working combined with Quinnine I was successful in warding it off. Not forgetting hot tea as a grand thing for perspiration.

157

Tuesday April 26ᵗʰ 81

Today I have been as usual running about and
looking after the hoe women. I also sowed some
onion bulbs and carrot and Linseed. I fear the drought
will put an end to them all before long however it is
but an experiment in a plot of moist soil. The tearing
down of the bush has been rather a stiff job owing to
thick and intertwined plants. Perserverance doubtless
will overcome the difficulty. In the evening I
purchased from Mr. Reid a pair of sleeping pajamers
[sic], clothe brush, a towel, and to the bargain got a
knife Gratis.

Wednesday April 27ᵗʰ 81

Making a prodigious effort I managed to get out of
bed about 6 o'clock. I called the roll and dispersed the
workers to the ground but I must admit the density of
the bush almost cut-off all access to the trees, however
by unwanted perseverance all hands got to work and

by night a pretty good clearance was made. The new cook house is making slow progress, but this is due to the fact that the wood for making it has be taken a good distance from the Station. Tonight the joiner boys have been in with us at lesson. I heard two of them read the lesson for the evening pretty well. A few others were engaged at Arithmetic with Mr. Reid.

Friday April 29th 81

This morning the warning drum was beaten before it was quite light. It had no effect on the people whatever, they did not make their appearance until it was just rather behind the time. A second pealing of the drum had to be resorted to and even then they were slow in coming. During all the time I was calling out the names a second time for the benefit of the late ones. During this forenoon two large venomous snakes were killed by the workers in the bush. They both measured about a yard long and one of them was as thick as my forearm while the other as thick as my wrist. I brought them up to the house and got one of the workman to give them a decent burial. After dinner time Mr. Reid and I repaired to the cook house and tried to refine 5 lbs of very brown sugar. The sugar was put into the pot with very little water. It soon melted and boiled and then it was syringed through cloth and the superfluous matter extracted from it—It was again reboiled and the same process was gone through. After two boilings [sic] it was allowed to cool, stirring it all the time. It is now six hours since the process was gone through and still the sugar has not solidified. The failure of the experiment is due to one or other of two causes or neither of them. The addition of water or inefficient boiling, our next experiment will cover both the previous supposed causes if nothing more is necessary. At sunset a runaway slave appeared at our door thinking of us that we would defend him against his master or chief whom he said sought his life, to take it to Mr. Reid felt for the poor fellow when he told him that the mission did not take to do with any native disturbance and that he could not be harboured by us. The young fellow separated to make the best of his condition.

> **Author comment:** It must be emphasized again that individual missions were under strict orders from the Foreign Missions Committees back home not to become involved in disputes such as these. As time passed, the European governments would demonstrate greater interest in asserting jurisdictional authority in these kind of disputes, with the intent of establishing who the supreme authority within any given protectorate, actually was. Sutherland has already described instances where the missionaries became involved in tribal matters spite of these prohibitions (see: 'Bill and the runaway wife,' entry dated April 2, 1881).

Saturday April 30th 81

This morning, after breakfast I counted out the yards of calico required for paying the work people. Today we paid over 900 yards of calico to 238 persons engaged at work on the Station the last fortnight. On the whole an amount of work was gone through with. The bush has been cleared for a considerable distance and now only waits the time when the fire shall be put to it. After we got through with the payments of Mr. Reid and I went down to the Lake and had a splendid bathe. For fear of crocodiles we did not venture far out but Right inshore. A proper rubbing with soap finished the exercise.

Sabbath May 1st 81

This morning when we rose news was awaiting us that two large elephants were not far distant from the Station and that they were destroying the gardens of the natives. Mr. Reid dispatched a few of his workmen with guns to ascertain their whereabouts and to bring back word. After a short while they returned having found no trace of them. During day of the neighboring Chiefs named Warenga came to help capture the elephants. Mr. Reid told him it was Sabbath day and that no shooting was done on that day but if they remain until tomorrow we shall hunt them. The Chief then said that they would be away by that time, and wished to go today. Mr. Reid did not comply with his wish, so no more was said. In the afternoon when Mr. Reid was away preaching at a village 2 miles from the Station he heard that there were no elephants to be seen and that the whole affair was a make up. As usual on the Sabbath Mr. Reid preached to a large gathering of natives who assembled in the front of the house. His subject was "Noah and the Ark." The people listened attentively to the story and those who knew the Chinaaja language carried the brunt of the sermon with them and could repeat parts of the story tolerably well afterwards.

Monday May 2nd 81

No word about the elephants today. If they paid a visit to the gardens of the natives yesterday there would be no end of complaints brought to us today. This morning I engaged 131 persons for the work on the Station during the next fortnight @ 4 yards of calico each @ 6 P [pence] a yard. I started the road this week again with a squad of 30 persons a few days more will finish as much of it as is lined off. Today has been very hot, especially on the road which is studded with brush on both sides. The clouds of dust that rose from the upturned earth made my position all the more precarious as it filled the nostrils and stuck hard and fast to the skin which was dripping with perspiration. After the days work is over I have to strip of [sic] my clothes and have a wash.

Tuesday May 3rd 81

Again all the road making. I am now putting the finishing touches on it. Three men and two women are selected for the purpose. I have another squad of

25 women clearing the brush, etc. This day like the previous.

Wednesday May 4th 81

How sweet and refreshing is my sleep every night. I have enjoyed almost unbroken slumbers since I came to Bandawe. Being out on the move during the day I often feel quite fatigued. Today I have been working on the road and finished 200 yards of it. The rays of the sun have been very hot and the dust of the road almost choking.

Thursday May 5th 81

Still on the road and making slow progress owing to the multifarious roots which is come into contact with by shovels. For me to work much is out of the question because of the heat combined with the dust is simply intolerable, as often as there is opportunity I get under the shade of a tree to escape the scorching rays of the sun but my composure does not last long as the untutored hands of the Yahi Tonga are not accustomed to keep a straight course. Today Mr. Reid had a _____[?] or rather a consultation with two chiefs who came to get a sanction from the mission to proclaim war against against another chief who had wounded one of his subjects with a spear. Mr. Reid as usual told them that we did not come here to settle their quarrels that they were to do that themselves. The chiefs were left rather disconcerted at this, and departed. A few words from Mr. Reid would settle the paltry affair but if this was done it would only open a way for continuous appeals from injured subjects on behalf of their rights. I transplanted some parsley which was in a rather precarious position near the house to the small plot of ground which I have set apart for a few vegetables. The coffee and Quarvas [?] plumbs which I had exposed to the South wind succumb to the cold but on transferring them to the shade the Quarvas budded anew but the coffee has not revived yet. This fact proves that the climate

166

in exposed parts is not adapted for these plants and it likewise proves that Bandawe is much cooler than Livingstonia for both plants alike prospered with any change of atmosphere. Today a lighted taper was put to the dried grass and bush which caused a fine conflagration. As usual I have on the road gaffering the [sic] workers but very slow progress is being made because of the roots of trees which almost defy the shovels. The action of the shovels discover the roots and by means of native axes the roots are out. I felt somewhat feverish today but abundance of walking about almost dissipated it. The Quinnine bottle was also resorted to.

Saturday May 7ʰ 81

I managed to get out of bed this morning at the streak of day and sounded the drum for muster. Afterwards I went to the goat house and counted the goats which number 16 old ones and 6 kids. I then went to the road to look after the squad. At 12 o'clock work was finished for the day and 18 men were paid 72 yds calico for their fortnights labour. In the afternoon I resorted to the Lake and had a nice bathe and a proper wash.

Monday May 9th 81

This morning I rose just as the drum was sounding for work. My first duty was to call the roll and then take on as many new hands as required. I intended to engage 30 men and women for the next fortnight but I could only get 22. The reason for this is quite plain for the previous Monday we could not give work to over 100 persons who came in to the Station. However we can jog along nicely with our present squads. A squad of women were set on to hoe the grass on the sites for the houses which has to be leveled down about 2 feet. Another squad are finishing the road, another at wood carving, and another plastering the joiners shop, which was commenced a month ago. Today an unexpected incident occurred. At dinner hour while the joiner boys were resting in their house a few of the Bandawe workers on the Station seated themselves beside them in their house. Such an intrusion displeased the Chinanja boys—for both tribes are at enmity with one another and like the Jews and Samaritans have no dealings with one another. The rightful occupants at once ordered the Yahi Tonga fellows to slip, one or two obeyed but one desisted in going. The Chinanja boys observing this united in full force and put him out. In the struggle the rebel got a few bounces on the face which disfigured him somewhat. This was an immediate cause of complaints so he came to settle the matter with us and said that he had been bad used by the boys. Mr. Reid sent for his apprentices to ascertaine the whole truth. They all said that he was put out because he would not go when he was told, but they denied bad using him. Mr. Reid could not settle the matter himself but sent the injured man to bring his chief that he might know how native law regarded such cases. The chief came and at the close of the day the offended and the offenders were seated on the ground. Mr. Reid stood in the centre and heard both sides of the case. The Yahi Tonga who were in the house unanimously declared that they were not in the house at all but that the injured fellow was interfered on the outside. This seemed strange to us. On the other hand the joiner declared also unanimously that the Yahi Tonga were in the house and that one of them on being told to go, deferred from going. They then combined and put him out and in no way intentionally injuring his person. Which of them were we to believe? Well, Mr. Reid referred to the Chief and asked him what was to be done. The Chief after giving an oration demanded eight yards of calico to be given his subject who was injured. Mr. Reid would not hear of this for the evidence of the Chinanja boys was sufficient to prove that the pursuit was in the house, etc. Mr. Reid in summing up told the Chief that he would fine his own boys taking the law in their own hands and putting the man out when should have been coming to him first, and further that he would fine the other person for going in to the house when he had no right to go. The Chief looked blank at this decision and arose to go and all his subjects with him, remarking as he went that if his men and the mission men met they would likely fight. Here the matter rests unsettled with the Chief but so far as we are concerned Mr. Reid is to take some pay of his work men for doing wrong, the proceeds of which goes for medicinal purposes.

Tuesday May 10th 81

This day has been uneventful. The usual routine has been gone through. There was nothing said today about the hubbub of yesterday. The Yahi Tonga who failed to carry his case yesterday was at his work as usual quite calmed down. The only cow we have is showing bad symptoms of illness. She is getting thinner daily. We conjecture that she has been bitten by the teetse fly. There is also a kid of the goats which has a diseased mouth, swelling and foaming. I can't find out the remedy for either case here.

Wednesday May 11th 81

Mr. Reid tried on his hand at sugar-making today. Having bought five stalks of cane for 3 P on the previous day Mr. Reid squeezed the juice out of his vise which amounted to half a pail full. Afterwards he boiled it on the fire until it had nearlly [sic] all evaporated but what was left—was pure and clean through still in a liquid state. To complete the process it is beyond our power. Never mind we have some syrup for the trouble taken with the squeezing of it. In the afternoon I get a few women on to level down the sites set apart for houses. Having no carts for carrying the earth and no boxes at my immediate disposal. I lashed a few pieces of wood together something like hand barrows which served the purpose tolerably well.

Thursday May 12th 81

This morning we were favoured with a nice shower of rain. It only lasted for a few minutes however, and an hour afterwards effects had passed away—the heat of the sun causing it to disappear quickly. I visited the small plot of wheat which was sown a week ago and found it to be in braider [?]. Its low lying position and nearness to the Lake will I hope favour its growth and maturity. The heat is very intense in the sun and the slightest manual labour enhances perspiration. Clouds of eatable insects have been seen like smoke passing over the Lake. The distant shores of the East Coast of the Lake present large columns of insects like clouds of smoke issuing from huge bonfires. When these flies (viz kungoo) rest on shore the natives catch them and eat them as food.

Friday May 13th 81

I rose this morning at the usual time but shortly afterwards I felt sickish and soon vomited. About 10 of the clock I turned in to bed feeling quite cold. I then got as many blankets as possible which were heaped upon me and in a very soon time the coldness was substituted with Excessive heat. I perspired a great deal which is the best means of getting rid of fever. In the afternoon I rose and went about my business and at night I felt quite well. Tonight one of the oxen was _____[?] by another having a good bounce on the ribs, which made him topple over on his side. My attention was arrested by the loud groans of the animal so I hastened for a light and went in to the barn and found him breathing hard. After a few struggles he regained his equilibrium. The offending ox was then tied up for the night—although formerly they all remained loose. One of the kids departed this life today. It suffered from disease in the mouth to which it eventually succumbed.

Saturday May 14th 81

This morning I got up at daybreak quite refreshed after a sound sleep. This being paid day I got the calico out for the work people and disposed of 528 yards to them for their fortnights work. In the afternoon Mr. Reid and I asconded the little hill near the Station. At the top we could hardly get a view of the surroundings because of the long grass. Myriads of Kungoo flies also _____[?] the park for us so that our visit was anything but enjoyable. A few boys who accompanied us caught the flies with their mouths open and ate them just because they could not help it and we had to do the same ourselves but ultimately the boys gathered them off the trees and ate them greedily. After staying for an hour on the summit we descended and made for the Station.

"The typical native diet was said to include Kungu flies, flying white ants, beetle grubs, caterpillars, and locusts, as well as agriculture products grown at the mission stations."

—*Daybreak in Livingstonia*, pp. 105–108.

Sabbath May 15ʰ 81

At the native service today conducted by Mr. Reid was seen the largest turn-out of people that ever occurred here and as Mr. Reid testifies, the largest he has ever seen in Africa, calculating roughly there would be about 400 present. The audience listened to Mr. Reid very attentively when he told them the story of Abraham and Lot and the destruction of Sodom and Gommorrah. The rest of the day passed very quickly. As usual Mr. Reid addressed his apprentices in the evening.

Monday May 16ᵗʰ 81

This morning I engaged a squad of 80 persons to
carry on the work of the next fortnight. Today one of
our Billy goats died. I made a post-mortem
examination of his body and found that the right lung
was a solid mass of disease. Other two goats are ill
tonight.

Tuesday May 17ᵗʰ 81

The usual routine of work has been carried on today.
The leveling process is progressing slowly and also
the Bush clearing. Tonight when the cattle came in
from grazing one of the oxen was ill, becoming nearly
unable to stand and breathing hard. While going
amonst the cattle which are all loose I received a blow
in the ribs from the heifer that made me look about
myself. No serious injury followed from the
unexpected _____[?] of the brute's hind legs.

Wednesday May 18ᵗʰ 81

This morning I slept in but made up for lost time by refraining from sounding the (ng--omo) drum at the halting hour. I sowed some Maize today in a plot of moist soil. The amount was only a few pounds as an experiment. The sick ox is much better today and has taken some oatmeal and Maize gruel, also some Cassaw [sp???] leaves. Some of the goats are lame, one or two of which is due to unequal cloves and another has got one of its hind legs strained. Tonight I am very tired indeed but I have ample rest in the house—from sunset to sunrise just about 12 hours.

Thursday May 19ᵗʰ 81

The ox is in a very declining state today. I have given up all hopes of recovery. He has been lying all day and not able to rise. His lower parts have swollen greatly and his breathing is quick. I have not been of much use today having to take to my bed for a few hours. Tonight I am restored to my usual health.

Friday May 20th 81

The ox was found dead in the morning. He was afterward dissected and his heart was found gorged with blood. One lung was a little affected with disease. The boys took care of the carcas [sic] and we kept his skin.

> *[Here the daily entries in the journal
> concludes, poetry follows]*

What cannot be mended must be borne
Risk nothing, nothing won
His life was gentle and the Elements
So mixed up in him, that Nature might
Stand up and say to all the world
This was a man.

—William Shakespeare

Who severe's not another's will
Whose armour is his thought
And simple truth his utmost skill

(2)

Who God doth take and early pray
More of his grace than gifts to lend
And entertain the harmless day
With a well chosen book or friend

(3)

Better than gold is a peaceful home
When all the fireside favourites come
The shrine of love the haven of life
Hallowed by mother, or sister, or wife
However humble that home may be
Or tried with sorrow by heaven's decree

a

The blessings that never were bought or sold
And centre there, are better than gold.

—Anonymous

There is a tide in the affairs of mentioning
Which taken at the flood leads on to fortune
Omit it all their future lives
Bound in shadows and mysteries.

—William Shakespeare

Obsta pinciplies, Resist the beginnings

James Sutherland's Grave
1857 – 1885
[unknown location]
Angoniland, British Central Africa

"The following letter has been received by the Wick Free Church Young Men's Christian Association from Dr. Elmslie, regarding the late Mr. James Sutherland, Livingstonia."

Angoniland
Livingstonia, Lake Nyasa
Eastern Central Africa
9th October, 1885

MY DEAR FRIENDS:

It behooves me as a member of your Society, as well as a warm personal friend of our departed brother James Sutherland, having seen his life and work in this dark land, to put on record in the society, my deep sense of the loss which not only we, but the church also, have sustained in his early death. As being associated with him for some months before his death in the work of the mission at his station, and as being engaged in furthering the work for which he has laid a good and sure foundation, I shall communicate to the committee my appreciation of his good and self-denying labours.

But he was distinctly one of ourselves, and as such we are bound to give thanks to God for him and for what he has been enabled to do in this land. Our president, Mr. Renny, will be able to go further back in his history than I can, and tell you of the dawning of the higher life in his soul, and with what fidelity and meekness he took up and continued to carry on his work in the vineyard of the Lord. My own acquaintance with our departed friend dates back to 1878, when as a youth of almost the same age we formed a close companionship and a friendship of the warmest kind, which has never been marred by any misunderstanding or difference of any kind. In my work in Wick, I had in him always a ready and efficient helper and in my studies and aspirations as an [?] associate. In our society meetings especially in the Sabbath morning fellowship meeting he was always in his place and held the esteem of us all. We doubtless remember the care devoted to the preparation in these meetings, and the warm, devotional spirit which he always evidenced in conducting the spiritual exercises in them. The superintendent of the Sabbath school in which he taught will be able to bear testimony to the punctuality and love for his work in that [?]. . . active member of the church and has left us a noble example. The work which he has been enabled to do in this heathen land has not been such a work as can be tabulated in a report and submitted to the General Assembly of the Church—it has been pioneering work and the laying of a foundation upon which those who come after him without fear of loss. None but those who have done such work can estimate the trying nature of each work—the gaining of the confidence of the people and the overcoming of their prejudices—the acquiring of unwritten languages—the all too uncomfortable housing, in the midst of that dread enemy malaria, and the call to act without advice and support in times of difficulty. Entering upon the work to which he had given himself at a time when the chief station of the mission was being removed from Cape McLear [sic] to Bandawe he endured the hardships of founding that station with no proper home in which to live and learned the language of the people which had not been written before. The laying out of the grounds of the station, the building of houses and the carrying on of work with lazy, willfully careless and insolent natives unaccustomed to work, was the task devolving upon our brother, calling for the greatest patience, self-denial, and ability to manage natives—a task which he carried out with efficiency and with pleasure to himself because he considered it God's work. He laid the foundation for the present successful work at Bandawe, and just at time when, with a full knowledge of the native language, he was delighting in the extensive opportunities for preaching the gospel to the people, he was sent to this tribe to open a new station and resume his former hardships of bad accommodations and the trials from a people considered by all to be the most unmanageable in all of Lake Nyassa. When asked if he would undertake this work—a solitary white man in the midst of a warrior tribe—he had no wish to choose his work, but to go and do whatever was allotted to him. His work at this station involved upon him, the acquiring of another unwritten language, and as he was about to be able [?] . . . the substantial and comfortable buildings to appropriate the wise care and ability with which this work has been done. I have but to think of the crowds of natives who have come to the station to get particulars of his death and to express their greatest sorrow that their friend and brother has been taken from them. From the chief to the meanest slave of the tribe, James Sutherland was held in regard and beloved by all. I have but to engage in worship with the natives and hear them sing our hymns and our tunes, to know the diligence with which he sought to teach them Scripture truths in song as well as in sermon. I have but to think of the many evenings that I have accompanied him to the villages and he would boast in enthusiasm how incessant were his labours for the evangelizing of all heathens. He has sown the good seed, and though he has not been permitted to see it ripening as fruit, the work is not lost and stationed now as I am with his foundation to build upon, to carry on the work here, I shall ever connect the devoted labours of our brother with the successes which I pray God may be pleased to grant me.

As a young missionary I have often been helped by the advice and wisdom of our brother, whose cheering companionship has made my task easy and my life here very happy. I cannot trust myself to speak of my sense of personal loss, but though a dark, dark cloud has passed over me, I am strengthened for work by my memories of him for whom today the heathen are mourning. Though, as I trust, our remembrance of [?] him will not end with this record of our loss, there is a memorial of him, than which no man desire a better, in that he lives in the hearts of the benighted people of this land. It has been denied his friends at home to minister to him in his last hours on earth, but could they but realize the widespread sorrow existing both here and at Bandawe, they would rejoice that God has so honoured him as to make his loss so widely felt. What can be more encouraging to me, whom am young in the service of the Lord in this field, than to know, as is now evidenced, that these heathen have hearts which are touched by sorrow as ours are, and that beneath the great mass of heathen superstition and ignorance there exists a hope here which will reciprocate the same quality in my behavior towards them as our brother's life, has proved [?] . . . It was the pleasure of the work that filled our brother's mind, and I remember the vehemence which he rebuked the weaklings who would cry out about the sacrifices made in living here. His principle was always the same—"What has Christ done for me? When I lay down my life in my work, I will still be a debtor to Christ. He has now done with the trials and hardships of this life; his days have been few, but his life is complete; he has done his work, and now rests. To us it is mysterious that a young life so full of promise for the future should be so soon ended by death; but it is the Lord, and He knows best. Our brother has been a faithful soldier of the cross, and has died at his post in the ranks of the few who are here enduring the heat and burden of the day in the war against this adamant heanthenism [sic]. We revere his memory, and give God thanks for what has been done through him.

I cannot close without asking you personally if you have given any attention to the earnest question of God's call for more labourers to go out to this vineyard. Think of this vast land and the now open highways of millions of people, of whom the Lord has said, "Other sheep I have which are not of this fold; them also I must bring, and they shall hear my voice." They are hearing His voice, because so few have heard it, and who enjoy its sweetness, are content to keep the blessing all to themselves. The heathen are our brothers; and here this day this vast tribe is mourning the loss of one of yourselves. They have heard from his lips the invitations of Christ; and now, who of you will take his place, and lead them into the full light of Christ's love? The cry is, "Son, go work today in my vineyard." If you are a son, seek guidance from the Master as to where he would send you; but work you must if you are a son. This tribe for whom James Sutherland labored so earnestly would occupy more than the county of Caithness and to all this people there are only three of us. How many Christian workers are there in Caithness for fewer people, most of whom can read the word of God themselves? Is the proportion just an arrangement? My warmest wishes to you all, and uniting with you in sorrow for our great loss.

I am yours, sincerely,

Walter A. Elmslie

> **Author comment**: remarkably, in the closing paragraph above, while reporting on James Sutherland's death, the author is at the same time recruiting his replacement.

FINAL NOTES

WILLIAM KOYI

a

James Sutherland's journal ends abruptly in the spring of 1881. He had been in Africa for less than six months. We are uncertain why his writing ended in the manner it did. Nor are we aware of any other journals written by Sutherland in Africa. We do know after arriving at Livingstonia I at Cape Maclear he was quickly reassigned to building Livingstonia II at Bandawe where he began performing a variety of daily tasks, and supervising teams of tribal members in their work around the new mission. A year later he was sent out from Bandawe to a remote village called Njuju, joining South African native missionary colleague William Koyi. Koyi was a critical link between the tribal members and the mission because he spoke several local Swahili dialects. Eight months after the death of James Sutherland, on June 4th 1886, Koyi succumbed to an unnamed tropical disease.[69]

Between his grinding work and attempts at learning native languages, it is unlikely Sutherland had time to reflect and write about his experiences. He was far too busy "doing." There is no evidence he kept any journal other than this one. Beyond his journal, all the primary documents we have before his death from tropical disease in Angoni-Land in late September 1885 are three letters he sent home to Scotland.

---

[69] *A History of African in Nyasaland*, 1875–1945, PHD thesis, Roderick J. Macdonald, University of Edinburgh, January 1969, pp.59-60.

More than 130 years of history separate us from James Sutherland and his time. We may find it convenient, from historical hindsight, to criticize Victorian morals and attitudes, but we would do well to recall our own history of late 19th century America. In 1898 America flexed her imperialist muscle by instigating war with Spain to challenge that country's tenuous grip on her overseas possessions. The Spanish-American War and the resulting territorial acquisitions from Spain was an impressive debut for the world's newest imperial power.

By the end of the 19th century America achieved her Manifest Destiny by exterminating or removing Native American tribes to remote reservations. In other parts of the world European explorers, missionaries, and armies were bringing 'Christianity, Commerce, and Civilization' to the indigenous peoples of Africa, India and China. In both situations, new technologies were used by the occupying powers' to subdue native resistance. Christianity and Social Darwinism was the justification for this unchecked demonstration of power.

In today's age of American so-called "exceptionalism," we should avoid casting stones from *our* twenty-first century glass houses. We can only speculate what future generations will make of our current tangled state of affairs in Iraq, Afghanistan, and Africa, and the political decisions and actions—misguided and otherwise—that brought us to where we are today.

Bibliography

Boahen, A. Adu, *African Perspectives on Colonialism*, the Johns Hopkins University Press, Baltimore, MD, 1987.

Brantlinger, Patrick, PHD, *Victorians and Africans: The Genealogy of the Myth of the Dark Continent*, Critical Inquiry 12, Autumn 1985, The University of Chicago Press.

Conrad, Joseph, *Heart of Darkness. Authoritative Text. Backgrounds and Contexts Criticism*, Paul B. Armstrong, ed., Brown University, W.W. Norton & Co., New York, New York, 4th edition, 2006.

Coupland, Sir Reginald, *The Exploitation of East Africa: 1856–1890*, Northwestern University Press, 1967.

Duncan, Graham A., *The Origins and Early Development of Scottish Presbyterianism in South Africa (1824 – 1865)*, Department of Church History and Polity, University of Pretoria, Pretoria, South Africa.

Elmslie, Walter A., *Among the Wild Ngoni*, Fleming H. Revell Co., Publishers of Evangelical Literature, NY – Chicago – Toronto, 1899.

Harrison, Eugene, "David Livingstone: The Pathfinder of Africa," from, *Giants of the Missionary Trial*, Worldwide Missions. On-line resource: www.wholesomeworlds.org.

Hastings, Adrian, *The Church in Africa: 1450–1950*, Oxford Scholarship on-line, www.oxfordscholarship.com, Published 1996.

Herman, Arthur, *How the Scots Invented the Modern World: The True Sotry of How Western Europe's Poorest Nation Created Our World & Everything In It*, Three Rivers Press, New York, 2001.

Hinflelaar, Maria, An Abstract: *Conflict and Protest in a Scottish Mission Area, North-eastern Zambia, 1870–1935*, Centre of African Studies, University of Edinburgh, 1994.

Hochschild, Adam, *King Leopold's Ghost: A Story of Greed, Terror, and Heroism in Colonial Africa*, Houghton-Mifflin Co., Boston – New York, 1999.

Iwenebor, Ehiedu E.G., *The Colonization of Africa*, New York Public Library, Schomburg Center for Research in Black Culture, Hunter College, (date unavailable).

Jack, James William, *Daybreak in Livingstonia: The Story of the Livingstonia Mission, British Central Africa*, Fleming H. Revel Co. NY, Chicago, Toronto, Publishers of Evangelical Literature, 1900.

Johnston, Sir Harry H., *British Central Africa: The Territories Under British Influence North of the Zambesi*, Metheun & Co., London, 1879.

Kwamena-Poh, M., Tosh, J., Waller, R., and Tidy, M. *African History in Maps*, Longman Group UK Limited, 1982.

Livingstone, W.P., *The Life of Robert Laws of Livingstonia: A Narrative of Missionary Adventure and Achievement*, George H. Doran, Co., New York. (date not available)

Macdonald, Roderick James, PHD Thesis, *A History of African in Nyasaland*, 1875–1945, University of Edinburgh, January 1969.

McCracken, Prof. John, *Politics and Christianity in Malawi 1875 – 1940: The Impact of the Livingstonia Mission in The Northern Provence*, Kachere Monograph No. 8, Kachere Series Zomba, Malawi, 2008.

Pakenham, Thomas, *The Scramble For Africa: White Man's Conquest of the Dark Continent From 1876–1912*, Random House, New York New York, 1991.

Rankin, Daniel J., *The Zambesi Basin and Nyassaland*, William Blackwood and Sons, Publisher, Edinburgh and London, 1893.

f

Roberts, John S., L.L.D., *The Life and Explorations of David Livingstone*, D. Lothrop & Co., Chicago, Belford, Clarke, & Co. 1881.

Schoefflers, Matthew, *Themes In The Christian History of Central Africa*, T.O. Ranger, Ed., University of California Press, Berkeley and Los Angeles, 1975.

Stewart, Dr. James, *Dawn in the Continent or Africa and Its Missions*, Fleming H. Revel Co. NY, Chicago, Toronto, 1903.

Waterson, Jane Elizabeth, *The Letters of Jane Elizabeth Waterson, 1866–1905*, The Van Riebeeck Society, Publisher, 1983.

Wilson, George Herbert, *A Missionary's Life in Nyasaland*, Isha Books, New DDA Market, New Gupa Colony, New Delhi India, First published 1920.

Appendix

Appendix I

Native Tribes Near Lake Nyasa

Appendix II

James Sutherland's Three Letters To Wick,
Scotland

Appendix III

Copy of Log of Livingstonia Missionary Personnel,
1874–1885

Appendix IV

Notes on African tropical diseases in Africa

Appendix V

Author Essay: "The Scramble for Africa: Explorers,
Traders, & Preachers"

APPENDIX I

Native Tribes Near Lake Nyasa

It is difficult to encapsulate the number and names of the various tribes, the many languages and dialects spoken, and the complex, ever-changing conflicts James Sutherland encountered serving as a missionary at the Livingstonia missions at Cape Maclear and Bandawe. Over 15 dialects were spoken in and around those missions alone. The four authors in this book's Bibliography offering, perhaps, the most comprehensive pictures of the cultures, languages, history, personalities, and religious beliefs of the tribes include James William Jack, Sir Harry Johnson, W.P. Livingstone, and George W. Wilson. Dr. Walter Elmslie's *Among the Ngoni* also deserves mention here.

In 1920, George Wilson, a missionary at the Universities Mission (Anglican Church, sponsor), wrote about his impressions of the people he knew and interacted with in 'Nyasaaland.' His views reflect the paternalistic attitudes of the Victorians from the previous generation:

> "There seem to me to be two special failings in the African character which constantly show themselves. I will mention these first and be done with them. In the first place the African seems to lack something, some stiffness of character, some backbone—I do not know what to call it . . . an example will best show what I mean. My teacher is a good fellow and has a real zeal for his work—I

speak generically—but if he happens to feel unwell in the morning he simply drops everything. He has certain quite important duties but he just lets them go—I suppose our religion and civilization have ground into us the importance of duty while the African does not yet feel a very strong sense of duty . . . The second failing comes as a great shock to one. At first one is struck by the very honest expression of the African face. As a matter of fact dishonesty, in word and deed, is a notable characteristic of the Central African folk. I say this very sadly with deep conviction. In village life I do not believe there is any disgrace attached to dishonesty unless it be found out."[70]

The Ngonis were considered the most influential (and most violent) tribe living near Lake Nyasa in the last two decades of the 19th century. Their traditional enemies were the Yaos, who allied with Arab slave traders for economic purposes. South of the Blantyre mission, in the Lower Shire region, the dominant tribe was the Makolos, at one-time close friends of David Livingstone after he gave them rifles to formalize relations with them. Livingstone engaged the Makolos' in part because they occupied a strategic position, blocking Portugese access to Lake Nyasa, (preventing Portugal's influence from spreading northward to Lake Nyasa). Livingstone was not merely on a mission of mercy for God.

---

[70] *A Missionary's Life in Nyasaland*, Geo. H Wilson, pp. 21 – 23.

j

Ngoni Warriors

Typical Ngoni Girls

k

James Sutherland documents an encounter with a Makolo Chief Maseha (see entry dated Feb 4, 1881), where the travelers bring fire arm gifts to him to ensure the continued safe passage of missionaries and supplies on the Shire River, up to Lake Nyasa. At the time the Makolo were sending their children to mission schools, but as the generation befriended by Livingstone died off, the once-strong alliance with the British withered, demonstrating that political, economic, and military arrangements (formal and otherwise) changed rapidly in the colonial period in Africa, including those between individual tribes, tribes and European powers, as well as among the imperial powers themselves. Like today, self-interest always was the driving force behind diplomacy, whether conducted by the western imperial powers or by local tribes living in and around Lake Nyasa.

Appendix II

Angoni Country Station
Livingstonia
August 15, 1882

My Dear Father:

After the lapse of another month I begin to
write home. You will observe by the
heading of this letter that I am not at
Bandawe. I told you in my last that I
intended going to these hills for a change so
here I am a distance of 57 miles from
Bandawe. Enjoying the best of health I am
the guest of Mr. Koyi who is now in sole
charge of the worke [sic] here. He has built
a house for himself at present but no
further steps are being taken yet in the way
of building a Station as section of the
Angoni tribe are unfavourable [sic] to us
settling in the country. The School was
staffed by command of the Lead Chief

Mombera about two months ago. The preaching of the Gospel is also limited to the village of one chief who is very friendly to us. But we have good hope that in a very soon time all the obstacles which at present keep us within narrow limits will be surmounted so that we shall have free and full access unto the working of the whole tribe. Barriers seem to give away everyday by noticing the manner and conduct of the people towards us. Since I came here 3 weeks ago it appeared as if we should have to shake the dust of our feet and leave. It so happened when Dr. Laws and Dr. Hannington were here that a son of the head chief and a Councillor died suddenly. A few ill-disposed persons got up the cry that the white man was the cause of these sudden death so that the mater came to a trial. The head chief Mombera and his many wives tried to question the others and to clear us of any blame. However, the

n

popular feeling had the better of Mombera and the matter had to submit to native trial. All the head men and Councillors were called to assemble when the usual mode of finding out the guilty parties was resorted to. Three fowls were selected, one to represent the Angoni tribe and one to represent the Arabs and the other to represent us. All three were put to the test and forced to swallow a certain quantity of the liquid poison called muave. The fowl representing the tribe died, the other two vomited so that we escaped what might have been our doom. The vomiting of the fowl says Mr. Koyi was the thin cord which kept us from our fate. It is a rude method of finding out the guilty, still it is native law. Thus, my situation for the first few days was rather unpleasant and Mr. Koyi felt it more so than I did as he knows the language and hears all the Talks that are continually taking place. Since then, however, the aspect of affairs are inclining more in our favour. The head chief Mombera is and has always been on our side but he is ruled by his head men, some of whom are usurpers to the chieftainship and wish to dethrone Mombera if they could. This is the people of whom I used to speak of in former letters as the dwellers of the hills, the terror of all their neighbours. At Bandawe we were kept in terror also by the Angoni, but now a temporary peace is established between the two tribes. The Angoni are of Zulu Kaffer [sp?] descent and have migrated in the course of time from there [sic] own Land in South Africa. In their wandering up country they suffered many divisions and split so that the other 5 sections of the Tribe are settled in Central Africa at remote distances from one another. They are a very brave and noble looking people and capable of becoming under the influences of the Gospel a people

p

much superior to many tribes in this region. They are ardently devoted to the cause of plunder and seem to be in their elements when making raids on their neighbours [sic].There [sic] Chief delight is in acquiring cattle of which in this locality there are hundreds. Here milk can be purchased for a trible so that we supply ourselves with plenty of butter. The country is also open and the weather home-like. Since I came here I have done very little worke [sic] having only built a chimney in the House with bricks so that we may warm ourselves in the Evening. The chimney stack protrudes through the roof and from the floor is 18 feet high. Many natives came to see the curiosity and expressed a sense of wonder at the smoke issuing from the roof. The present place is only to be temporary as a better site has not yet been found. Much worke (sic) is not to be preceeded with at present until the people are settled down to know our ways and desire us always to stay among them. It touched their national pride when we first built Houses among the Atonga tribe who were until 5 years ago their slaves. And now they would have us to leave the Atonga and come and stay among them altogether. It is absolutely necessary that a white man should be here always or else the people will say that we came to stay a short while with them, then go away and deceive them. This happened a few years ago with the mission so that mission withdrew from another part of this country and did not let the people know they were going. They are afraid we will do the same again when the mission party first came into this country Mombera promised them an 11 herd of cattle in his Country. It looked not long ago as if the mission had forfeited that generous gift but of late the chief has revised the subject to Mr. Koyi and Mr. Koyi has heard since that the chief

& his headmen have decided to give us the cattle so that there are yet some gleams of hope for to establish our mission here. The friendship of the head chief is apparently getting firmer the longer we stay but he will not hear of us starting a school. There are so many superstitions among them that they are afraid we will bewitch them. Their worship of which they have a form consists in the worship of their forefathers spirits. The Word of God is new to them and after hearing it the young men collect together to talk about the New Religion. They reason under the dim light which has come down to them hereditary. They argue that the worship that has come down to them through past generations and which they inherited from their fathers must have been the same from the beginning and that God ordered it so that the Sins and Evil deeds which they have committed have also come down to them. Here Mr. Koyi comes in

S

& tells them to worship the true & one God who made them & made all things which they see and possess. They admit that it is the best way to worship. Thus the latent powers of some of the Angonies are waking up to consider their condition. We do fondly hope & trust that the day is not far distant when this people will surrender themselves to the reception of the good news which we bring into their Land.

Yesterday the 25th of August our mails arrived from Bandawe. We were cheered to see letters & papers from Home. I received two letters from you, those of April & May and one letter from Mr. Robertson--Traffic Agent--I was glad to hear so much good news and see how things are moving in the Home [unintelligible] Changes are ever taking place. I was glad to hear about the Peat Cutting and the Singing of the Watten Ladies. What of Solos & Duets and Songs &

t

Speeches and what more have been taking place among the celebrities of far fumed Watten [?] It was rather cheering to see so many well know names taking part in the programme of the Evening. What bas become of John Basin? Off [sic] course he was there. Surely he was not a whit behind in the display of his musical talents. I am sure he is not bashful at least I thought so and certainly the Ladies don't thinke [sic] him so. Perhaps you forgot, so tell him he acquitted himself. I was glad to see R. Setons name also taking part in Hearts of Clark, but I have forgotten him in not answering his letter.

In my letter to Alec Sutherland of September last year I had some words for him but that letter never reached. I have not got over the List of my correspondents yet but I hope to write him soon. You enquire after my boots. I am just about run

u

out so that I must take to mending of them. I would be glad to get a few pairs out, say 1 pr of Clarence Boots which are very handy here and 2 pairs of Lacing Boots half watertight with iron heels & plenty of spring in the soles but no [unintelligible]. Also a pair or two of slippers. My stockings are also getting a fright though I had about a dozen pairs from Capt Fairley before he left. You might give Aunt $L 2 [two pounds] and bid her work some stockings for me not very heavy ones. I am very hard on stockings seeing that my duties keep me always on foot.

I would also require a few worsted shirts. You need not expect that the Mission will bring out these articles for me as Mission goods. You may get it out along with mission goods in a separate [sic] box for a distinct individual having to pay the cost & run the riske. The expenses will exceed the value of the whole contents but send it out by all means. You speake of me of having had Debts and that Fairley owes me $L6 [six pounds]. I received a good many articles from him in kind which I thought settled that difference. So I think his $L6 is a gast [?] - But when I get it he will explain matters. Dr. Laws asks is the Man in his senses when he heard of the Man [unintelligible] again. Dr. Laws has returned with the steamer after seeing Dr. Hannington past Blantyre. [Unintelligible] 6 penny note Books in the Box which you sent. I have now done. Remember me to my inquiring friends.

I remain
Your affectionate Son

James Sutherland

Angoni Country Station
Livingstonia
September 20, 1883

My Dear Brother:

It is such a very long time now since I
received your welcome letter that I forgot
the date yet I have no doubt you have
heard pretty frequently of my doings from
home, where I make it a point to write
every mail. I heard last mail that you were
thinking of going to Australia. I can by no
means find fault with you though father
says that you can rise in Glasgow as well as
in a foreign land. It is quite natural to
think so, but if I stayed in Wick or even in
Watten, do you or any other body think I
would receive a salary of $ L 140 [140
pounds] a year. I am cheated if they do. I
am glad I left Wick just for the sake of the
pounds, shillings, and pence, and if you

think or hope to better yourself by going abroad by all means go. But your case is different far from mine. I set out to a place cut and ready for me so that I had no dark thoughts of what I was to do. But on the other hand you are going out in a sense not knowing where you are going or what you are to do, so therefore you will leave home with very different feelings from me. I never was happier all my life than when I launched forth on the broad ocean and the same happiness continues to this very day unbroken and undisturbed. I don't expect this letter will find you in Glasgow and perhaps now you are away.

I am now up among the hills again among the Angoni people fully sixty miles inland from the Lake. Last year I had four months of the hills doing nothing, now as the people are receiving us I have commenced building a large brick house which must

y

be roofed before December. I am to be stationed here in this healthy country, so that whenever the King gives his sanction to open a school I am to be placed in it as teacher. I am learning the Kaffir language, after having a trail of two other languages on the Lake. In another month three years out the five will have expired. How quickly these years have fled past.

Since this year came in every Sabbath up to the middle of August I wrote Dr. Laws weekly sermons in short hand and then transcribed them for him for which he gave me five shillings each sermon. In all, I got $ L 8 [8 pounds] from him for sermons. He then engaged me to write a Ishinyanja Grammar in shorthand when he dictated it, I was engaged about an hour a night for three weeks, for which he gave me $ L 2 [2 pounds].See that I had to come to Africa to be paid for my shorthand. This sum made

z

this year's salary up to $ L 145 [145 pounds]. He was very extravagant in his living and left much debt both in the Mission and in the African Lakes Co.

The Blantyre Mission has had also a sad time of it in the deaths of Mrs. Duncan, wife of the gardner and Mrs. Nicol, wife of the teacher. It was with Mrs. Duncan that I stayed when I passed through Blantyre and I have a very lively recollection of their kindness and now that she's gone she is deeply and justly regretted. The wife of the teacher, Mrs, Niccol, was only one day in Blantyre when she took ill. She died [unintelligible] at the beginning of her career and Blantyre escaped. Now Blantyre has the reaction. Dr. Hannington had a narrow enough escape here last year. I have had only one severe sickness in Africa and that was when Capt. Fairley left in 1881. I have had splendid health ever since with occasional fevers. I think sometimes that I am intended for this country and this country alone. So that I may spend my days in it. However, I hope to go to Scotland in two years. I expect Mr. Elmslie [a man who later wrote James Sutherland's epitaph in the local papers back home in Scotland] out here next year. If he gets through his studies. I often think of studying when I go home by Medicine, but I doubt too much of my life is passed now for study. I will see, however. If I were to go home now I would have to pay my passage $ L 33 [33 pounds] from Quilemaine. In two years after this I will have a free passage home. I intend to stay. You may be sure especially as my health is excellent. I had a long letter from Bill Tast recently. He is doing well in Calcutta. He told me that Dr. Ross is to be married soon. I have now done. I remain your affectionate brother.

Jas. Sutherland.

Angoni Country Station
Livingstonia
September, 1884

My Dear Brother:

It is now a long time since I received your
letter from your new sphere. I must try now
to answer you. According to home accounts
you are getting on very well. It is a very
pleasant thought to have bright prospects
before us. I will have entered my fifth year
long before you get this. That is a pleasant
prospect indeed. After I came into the
country five years looked long enough, but
plenty of work made the time fly. The
climate is now beginning to tell on my
constitution and a good deal of my old
strength is gone. I am suffering under a
heavy cold just now, which I must be very
careful of. You will have heard by this
time that Mr. Elmslie now Dr. Elmslie has

been appointed for Livingstonia. I don't know yet which station he may be appointed to. If not for here, I will have a poor chance of seeing him as he will likely go to the North end of the Lake Station. If he is married he will likely have a salary of $ L 300 [300 pounds], if unmarried $ L 250 [250 pounds]. Were I coming out again in the same capacity of Agriculturalist, the Committee might give me $ L 160 [160 pounds]. So you see the difference a Doctor makes. I have no desire to be a Doctor for I don't think I would like it. I am now placed here as Teacher but the chief of this tribe will not allow us to teach though he allows us to preach. Therefore I am only a teacher in name. In reality I am a bricklayer & house builder for that is the kind of work at which I am engaged, and have been working at since I came into the country. Here we must put our hands to anything and everything just as it is required. You,

dd

on the other hand, will be kept at one particular branch of work with perhaps a change occasionally. If I had to stay at home through ill health or some other cause I don't know what I might do. To work much is out of the question and to beg I am ashamed. I think I hear a voice saying, As thy days so shall thy strength be.

Father is very particular now in telling me in his letters that he is growing old. He feels very much the absence of us all though he does not say it in these exact words. I am glad that is getting something to do in his new branch of trade. He says his old customers are coming gradually back. He still keeps by his half holidays. Many a time I tried to put him from it, but it was no go. He would rather loose [sic] a diet of meat than part with his Saturday afternoon. I don't know if his appeal to the public would have much affect on the

working men as they spend their money on
Saturday evening. Dugald I am told is
studying for the Civil Service. I think he
will find it very stiff work. He is also on
the outlook for another office. As his
present employers have no work for him. I
wonder what like he is now [?].Has he
grown much I fear he will be but dwarfish
at best. You see what his poor upbringing
on tea has done for him. I am glad I got a
start in growth before the hard pinching
days came, and they were really hard. I can
afford to cry out against them now but not
then. "Hard times come again no more."

Here sometimes no food can be got for
money, but then no money could be got for
food. If I am spared to go home I will make
a change in some ways in our home by
making it more comfortable. I must now

ff

conclude, hoping to hear from you before I leave Africa.

I remain your affec. brother.

Jas. Sutherland.

APPENDIX III

Roster of missionaries at Livingstonia Station, 1875–1890.
From Appendix of *Daybreak in Livingstonia*. James
Sutherland is listed as "Died, 1885."

Appointed		Missionaries.	Remarks.
1876	14	*William Koyi,*	Died, 1886.
1876	15	*Shadrach Ngunana,* Kafirs	Died, 1877.
1876	16	*A. Mapas Ntintili,* from Lovedale	Invalided, 1880. Died, 1897.
1876	17	Isaac Williams Wauchope,	Invalided, 1877. Now ordained pastor.
1877	18	*James Stewart,* C.E., F.R.G.S.	Died, 1883.
1878	19	*George Beuzie,* Master of *Ilala*	Died, 1880.
1878	20	Robert Reid, Carpenter	Invalided, 1881.
1878	21	J. A. Paterson, Engineer	Resigned, 1881.
1878	22	William B. Reid, Seaman	Resigned, 1881.
1879	23	Miss Waterston, M.D.	Resigned, 1880. Now in Cape Town.
1880	24	*James Sutherland,* Agriculturist	Died, 1885.
1880	25	George Fairley, Master of *Ilala*	Invalided, 1882.
1880	26	William Harkess, Engineer of *Ilala*	Joined A. L. Co., 1882.
1881	27	*R. Gowans,* Master of *Ilala.*	Died, 1883.
1881	28	John A. Smith, Teacher	Blantyre Mission.
1881	29	*Peter M'Callum,* Carpenter (Mrs M'Callum)	Bandawé.
1881	30	Rev. Robert Hannington, M.B., C.M.	Invalided, 1882. Now in Constantinople.
1881	31	Donald Munro, Builder	Invalided, 1885.
1882	32	George Williams (Kafir from Lovedale)	Resigned, 1888.
1883	33	*Rev. J. Alexander Bain,* M.A.	Died, 1889.
1883	34	William Scott, M.B., C.M.	Invalided, 1886.
1884	35	*William O. M'Ewen,* C.E.	Died, 1885.
1884	36	*Rev. Walter A. Elmslie,* M.B., C.M., F.R.G.S. (Mrs Elmslie)	Ekwendeni, Ngoniland.
1885	37	Rev. D. Kerr Cross, M.B., C.M. (Mrs Kerr Cross)	Resigned, 1896. Now in the Administration Service.
1885	38	*Mrs Kerr Cross* (the first)	Died, 1886.
1885	38	*George A. Rollo,* Teacher	Died, Dec. 1885.
1886	39	*Hugh Macintosh,* Carpenter	Died, Jan. 1887.
1886	40	*Maurice M'Intyre,* Teacher	Died, 1890.
1886	41	John B. M'Currie, Teacher.	Resigned, 1887.
1886	42	Robert Gossip, Bookkeeper	Invalided. Now under A. L. Co., Glasgow.
1887	43	*Rev. George Henry,* M.A., M.B., C.M.	Died, 1893.
1887		*Mrs Henry.*	Died, 1892.
1887	44	Charles Stuart, Teacher	Invalided, 1900.
1888	45	*William M'Kay Murray,* Carpenter	Livingstonia.
1889	46	*William Thomson,* Printer (Mrs Thomson)	Livingstonia.
1890	47	*Rev. George Steele,* M.B., C.M.	Died, 1895.
1890	48	*James H. Aitken,* Teacher	Died, 1894.
1890	49	George Aitken (*Mrs Aitken*)	Invalided, 1898.
1890	50	Rev. D. Fotheringham, M.B., C.M.	Resigned, 1893.

APPENDIX IV

Notes on African Tropical Diseases [c.1906]

"The only serious drawback to British Central Africa as a field of enterprise for trader or planter is malarial fever, either in its ordinary form, or in its serverest [sic] type which is commonly known as black-water fever.... Whether the development of medical science will enable us to find the same antidote to malarial fever as we have found for small-pox in vaccination, or whether drugs will be discovered which will make the treatment of the disease and recovery therefrom almost certain, remains to be seen. If however here, as in other parts of tropical Africa, this demon could be conjured, beyond all question the prosperity of Western Africa, or the Congo Basin, and of British Central Africa would be almost unbounded. Ordinary malarial fever is serious but not so dangerous as that special form of it which is styled "black-water," or haematuric. [sic] The difference between the effects of the two diseases is this. Ordinary malarial fever is seldom immediately fatal but after continued attacks the patient is often left with some permanent weakness. Black-water fever is either fatal in a very few days or has such a weakening effect on the heart that the patient dies during convalescence from sudden syncope..."[71]

---

[71] *British Central Africa,* Sir Harry H. Johnston, 1906, Methuen & Co., London, 3rd edition, pp. 178–9.

The Scramble for Africa:
Explorers, Traders, and Preachers

By Rod Haynes

"There is no evidence that missionary growth in central or west Africa was in expectation of a European take-over. It was, on the contrary, very clearly to uncolonial [sic] Africa they had gone. If we cut off the story at this point [late 1880s] there is adequate evidence across more than three-quarters of a century for the interaction of missionaries with an Africa outside colonial control—from Kuruman [South Africa] and Ibadan [Nigeria] to Livingstonia [Malawi] and Bugunda [Uganda]."

—*The Church In Africa* 1450–1950, Adrian Hastings, © 1996, p.258.

History is the story of human manipulation of political, economic, and/or military power, and the outcomes of those actions, good or bad. Our ability to accurately predict results of power projection remains an imperfect science today, in spite of all the twenty first century technology at our disposal. If nothing else history tells us that unexpected consequences can always be expected when power—in any form—is exercised.

The story of colonialism in Africa—and the first of two global conflicts that partially resulted from the Scramble for Africa less than two decades later—is a testament to our inability to control the future, regardless of the influence we *believe* we can impart. No one predicted the level of carnage visited upon the world by World War I. Just as importantly, the 'War to End All Wars' did not prevent an even more catastrophic global conflagration 20 years later.

Divergent forces were at work in colonial Africa in the 1870s and 1880s. Preaching the 'Word of God' to tribal members until his death, David Livingstone's achievements in exploring and mapping the interior of southern Africa where few (if any) white men had gone before are indisputable. Nevertheless, Livingstone should be considered an early imperialist. The same cannot be said of James Sutherland and others who followed in Livingstone's footsteps. Dissecting the motivations of Sutherland and other missionaries in the pre-scramble period are a separate concern from analyzing how David Livingstone laid the groundwork for the Scramble for Africa, though the two historical events unquestionably are related to each other.

The work of the missionaries unwittingly contributed to the Berlin Conference of 1884. The resulting scramble should still be viewed as an *unintended* consequence of the early missionary work of the European churches in Africa. Once the missionaries pried the door

kk

open by establishing missions and building relations with local tribes, a flood of commercial interests and European military forces poured in afterwards (at different times in different places on the continent). The missionaries then had no choice but to accept the new objectives imposed by Foreign Service Offices back home.

Nationalism and evangelism were two core cultural forces underpinning the Victorian age, characterized by feelings of racial superiority rooted in Social Darwinism. Some historians today claim that Scottish missionaries were less prejudiced than their English and other European counterparts, but the evidence suggests otherwise. Imperialism was a competition between western nation-states, fueled by a belief in the survival of the fittest humans at the expense of lesser humans, including—the vast majority of Victorians believed—native Africans, East Indians, and the Chinese. The Scots were *not* above holding paternalistic attitudes towards these Third World peoples.

The development of new weapons and communication technologies, new medicines, and other industrial age innovations fed the ambitions of the imperialists. Social Darwinism became a justification for the Scramble for Africa. Without invitation, Europeans took on what Rudyard Kipling labeled "the white man's burden" of freeing their African brethren from their witchcraft-based cultures and sadistic cruelty to neighboring tribes, including the slave trade. The Victorians believed the situations in India, China, and Africa required the kind of intervention only they could render. This belief fueled David Livingstone's vision of

Commerce, Christianity, and [European] Culture, his model to supplant the Godless slave trade industry.

In the wake of the scramble, James Stewart, a university-trained medical doctor and missionary in Africa (he was a co-founder of Livingstonia at Cape Maclear in 1874), denied that the missionaries were willing accomplices in the scramble. But their *contributions* to imperialism in Africa, intentional or otherwise, was self-evident:

> "The general sequence or order was there, as it has been elsewhere—the Explorer, the Missionary, the Trader, the administrator. The explorer goes, but returns soon, the missionary goes to stay, and he is followed by the other two, who also stay. We may accept this as true in the order of time, except that the first and second, Explorer and Missionary, are sometimes transposed, and at other times are combined. The aim of each is entirely different, but each of them aids in bringing about a new and better state of things … the belief is still held by some that there is a direct and designed connection between the territorial expansion of the [British] empire and missionary work. As against British Protestant Missions, the charge is unfounded."

> —*Dawn in the Dark Continent*,
> James Stewart, p. 211.

mm

Sir Harry Johnston, the British Consulate in British Central Africa/Nyasaland during the scramble, wrote an influential book with strong political overtones about his African experiences. Topics included African botany, the cultural habits of individual tribes, specific tribal languages and dialects, the complex imperial power posturing during the scramble, some unique characteristics and practices of the missionary movement, and more. Inherent biases aside, the book offers 21st century readers a comprehensive picture of what was going on in British Central Africa in the final quarter of the 19th century. It is one valuable primary source authored by a direct participant in the scramble.

In the opening pages of *British Central Africa: The Territories Under British Influence North of the Zambesi*, Johnston discusses the differences between protectorates, spheres of influence, and colonial possessions. A protectorate like British Central Africa in the late 1880s was a defined territory with set borders administered by government. Johnston served Britain as a Consulate there in the 1890s. A sphere of influence was much larger than a protectorate, having less defined boundaries with the responsibility for governing tribal members inhabiting the spheres less clear. Over the twenty five years preceding the scramble, Britain and Portugal had exchanged differing opinions—for the most part without resorting to violence—over who should control the sphere of influence in the region from the southern-most shores of Lake Nyasa (Cape Maclear, site of Livingstonia I) south to where the land bordered the Zambesi River. Clear lines of governance were not in place, with multiple church missions from different European powers dotting the landscape, and explorers and political representatives trying at various times and in different ways to establish treaties with the indigenous tribes around them. It later turned out Portugal's sphere of influence now known as Mozambique included almost all the area between the Zambesi and Upper Shire near the Blantyre Mission.

Prior to 1884, Portugal and Britain could not agree on the ownership of certain parts of African territory and the people occupying these lands. Great Britain's position was that *effective occupation* should be the governing principle of ownership, where Portugal claimed ownership under the concept of, *discovery territory*. Under the discovery principle, Portugal insisted that their explorers had been present in the territory stretching from the southern shores of Lake Nyasa, through the Shire River basin, to the Zambesi and beyond, long before the British arrived there. Portugal claimed the rights of ownership for this reason.[72] While Portugal's being there first was indisputable (and the British acknowledged as much), Britain did not subscribe to the principle of discovery territory. They had since arrived and had made their presence known locally among the tribal members by establishing missions, signing agreements with tribal

---

[72] It was noted earlier in this book that Mozambique was a penal colony for Portugal, in a real sense a dumping ground for convicts, akin to how Australia was once used by England.

chiefs, and cooperating with small trading outlets owned by European entrepreneurs. British explorers, missionaries, or commercial interests 'effectively occupied' these lands. Who had been there *first* was, in the eyes of the British, not relevant. The squabbling continued.

The Berlin Conference permanently altered the dynamics of this and other colonial ownership disagreements, to the detriment of Portugal's imperial aspirations. In late 1884, Bismarck called representatives of the colonial powers to Berlin where a formal agreement was hammered out and signed by all participants, including Portugal and Britain. Under Article 35 of the agreement the powers agreed to follow set procedures to avoid conflicts, specifically:

(1) Before a power made a claim to a territory, all parties (powers) must be notified of the pending claim;

(2) All claims to territory should be followed by annexation and *effective occupation*;

(3) Treaties signed with African leaders are considered legitimate titles to sovereignty for the signatories;

(4) Each power was allowed to extend coastal possessions to establish spheres of influence.[73]

---

[73] *African Perspectives on Colonialism*, p. 33

African Kings and tribal Chieftains were, of course, not invited to the Berlin Conference. The Conference decreed effective occupation, *not* discovery territory, defined a powers' right of possession, to the chagrin of Portugal. Aside from affirming the secret agenda of King Leopold of Belgium, effective occupation was the single most important governing principle agreed to at the Berlin Conference. A power (like Great Britain) could claim "effective occupation" if they could legitimately demonstrate:

> (1) Treaties had been established with local leaders;

> (2) The occupier was permitted to fly their national flag in these claimed territories;

> (3) Once an occupier established an administration in the territory with a police force, effective occupation had occurred.[74]

The Berlin Conference of 1884 is generally considered the official starting point of the Scramble for Africa. But there was no *definitive* starting date for the simple reason that not everything related to the occupying powers' assertion of sovereignty happened simultaneously in South Africa, British Central Africa, North Africa, and in the Congo, among all the other areas. The Conference was an attempt

---

[74]   Ibid.

to establish due process among the imperial powers as the scramble heated up. Avoiding armed conflict was a paramount goal of Conference leaders like King Leopold of Belgium. The Conference set ground rules in a region (Africa) that up to that point in time had little real, formal governance.

Professor A. Adu Boahen notes that, in the middle of the 19th century, a strong tide of individual national consciousness spread throughout Europe, coupled with a strong religious awakening among the masses. These movements encouraged feelings of greatness in the Foreign Service Offices of the imperial powers; these forces helped Bismarck unify Germany and then crush France in the Franco – Prussian War. A need for security accompanied the rise of industrialization and urbanization, whose products included surplus labor and tremendous population growth. European commercial interests sought new trading partners and new sources of raw materials. In the last few decades of the 19th century, Professor Boahen notes that the number of overseas colonies a nation possessed became a measure, or a *symbol*, of its prestige or greatness, a measure of its power, in essence a zero-sum game between individual powers. In the simplest terms a European power's status or standing in the world was increasingly defined by the number of overseas possessions she claimed for her own. These stirrings would eventually result in a brutal global conflict between the imperial powers within the next two decades.

James Stewart, a co-founder of Livingstonia who later remained in Africa to watch the early stages of the

Scramble for Africa unfold, anticipated Professor Boahen's observations about the scramble made decades after Stewart's work *Dawn in the Dark Continent* appeared in 1903:

> "The causes which led to the great partition [Scramble for Africa] were not one but many. National rivalries, jealousy, and greed; desire for territorial expansion, for colonies to absorb surplus populations and surplus manufactures, and an exaggerated idea of the probable immediate value of these new territories were all at work."

Perhaps Stewart had regrets about having a direct hand in the imperial powers' success in Africa. Not long after Livingstone was laid to rest at Westminster Abbey in the spring of 1874, Stewart encouraged the Foreign Missions Committee of the Free Church of Scotland to establish the first Livingstonia mission at Cape Maclear. It would help make Livingstone's 3-Cs a reality in the region between Lake Nyasa and the Zambesi River. The Committee endorsed Stewart's vision and the funding for the mission project was quickly raised among private supporters.

In hindsight, a blurring between the role of the missionaries and the effects of imperialism in the 1880s and 1890s was inevitable. The fierce Ngoni tribe was probably the single most powerful antagonist in the Lake Nyasa region. Over the years their raids had decimated their rival Tonga tribe and other neighboring tribes. The missions were not always successful in maintaining their neutrality between ancient rivalries in their attempts at keeping the peace. The missions were prohibited by their respective church sponsors from offering sanctuary to runaway slaves and warned not to adjudicate tribal disputes on missionary grounds (Foreign Service Offices agreed that this was not the role of missionary personnel and should be avoided at all costs). As time passed native troops supported by the European governments policed whatever vestiges of the slave trade remained to tamp down conflict between local tribes. This resulted in territorial claims by European foreign offices, claims that after the Berlin Conference of 1884 were evolving into formal colonial possessions, which the presence of native troops and police forces helped solidify. Western advances in medicine (quinine for example) were able to combat the deadly jungle diseases that wiped out a number of early missionaries, helped stabilize the personal health of missionaries that followed later. Steamships, telegraphs, railroads, and breech-loading rifles all tipped the technological scale to the advantage of the Europeans. Whatever resistance the tribal members offered as colonialism intensified, violent or otherwise, had little real chance of succeeding.

Once the colonies were identified and geographic boundaries more firmly established (and natives for the most part "conquered,"), further headway was achieved in converting the locals to Christianity. A modern history text notes:

"The impact of the missionaries varied considerably. Many of them tried to build up Christian communities composed of freed slaves and other refugees; individual converts could be made by this method, but at the cost of leaving African society unaffected . . . few missionaries advocated colonial rule, but their activities did have a bearing on the European partition from 1875 onwards. The missionaries were a source of information about local conditions; and they were used by their home governments to support "claims" to African territory. It was only after colonial rule had missionaries achieved their full impact on spiritual life and education."

> --*African History in Maps*, Kwamena-poh, Tosh, Waller, and Tidy, Longman Group UK, 1982.

In 1985 Dr. Patrick Balinger suggested a value shift in economic classes in Victorian Britain may explain a change in emphasis away from the progress of the missionaries towards satisfying imperial appetites:

"The transition from the altruism of the anti-slavery movement to the cynicism of empire building involved a transvulation of values .

. . For middle and upper class Victorians
dominant over a vast working class majority
at home and over increasing millions of
"uncivilized" peoples of inferior races
abroad, power was self-validating. There
might be many stages of social evolution
and many seemingly bizarre customs and
"superstitions" in the world, but there was
only one "civilization," one path of
"progress," one "true religion."[75]

The British and Scottish Royal Geographic Societies
continued their practice, begun in the era of David
Livingstone, of bringing the accomplishments of explorers
and missionaries before the public in Britain and Scotland.
Speeches, awards, publications of charts, and the growing
demand for more fed the Scramble for Africa. The same
thing happened at the same time in other parts of Europe.
The relationships between exploration and commerce, and
exploration and Christianity, and commerce and
Christianity, blurred further as the Scramble for Africa
moved towards its conclusion. Establishing an effective
colonial presence required a successful consolidation of
power and forced conformance to authority, goals shared

---

[75] *Victorians and Africans: The Genealogy of the Myth of the Dark
    Continent*, Critical Inquiry 12, Patrick Brantlinger, PHD,
    Autumn 1985, The University of Chicago Press, p.166.

by all the occupying powers in Africa in the late 19th century.

To suggest that the missionaries who followed James Sutherland into British Central Africa and in other places had little impact on the Scramble for Africa is to ignore what happened there. Whatever their original intentions, especially in the early days, the missionaries had a hand in making the lives of the Africans more miserable as the scramble ramped up. Many commercial interests from Europe were involved in the scramble, more so in some places like the Belgian Congo where King Leopold's exploitation of the tribal members became legendary by 1910. Writing about the informal partnership between the Livingstonia Mission (and others) and the African Lakes Company in the late 1870s and early 1880s, Daniel Rankin observed:

> "This eccentric attempt to combine the hetegenuous offices of priest and trader were met with little success financially and gradually devolved into a transport agency for the various local missions ... [but] it is to the missions we owe the roads and facilities of communication that have been so effectuated in the opening up of this large region. Indeed, the colony [Nyassaland] itself may almost be said to owe its existence to the indomitable determination

of these pioneers during the critical stages of
its early history."

—Rankin, *Zambesi Basin and Nyassaland*,
pp. 257-8.

The missionaries converted more tribal members than ever
before in part by building satellite missions in the brush and
having medical doctors introduce modern medicine to tribal
members. The Christian movement in Africa continued to
gain momentum as the 19th century drew to a close.

About the Author

Rod Haynes is a native Rhode Islander, holding degrees from Ripon College and Boston University. He has written two memoirs, ROGUES ISLAND MEMOIR (2001), and its sequel, 100 BOWEN STREET (2003). ZOEY'S TALES AND OTHER SHORT STORIES (2012) was Rod's first work of fiction. More information about these books can be found at www.highlanderpress.com. A third memoir about his ten years in the United States Navy is now in production. Rod works for the federal government in Seattle and is a part-time Adjunct Instructor of U.S. History at Green River Community College in Auburn, WA. He lives in Renton, WA with his wife Daria. They have four adult children between them.

Contact Rod at LIMEROCKER1@yahoo.com

Readers are encouraged to visit Rod's author page at www.amazon.com to offer constructive criticism of his work. Thank you for your interest.

Made in the USA
Charleston, SC
05 January 2016